T0117620

Bringing Mind Training to Life
An Exploration of the 5th Shamarpa's
Concise Lojong Manual   .

A Book by Shamar Rinpoche

Series

Bird
of
Paradise
Press

ABOUT BIRD OF PARADISE PRESS
Bird of Paradise Press is a non-profit book publisher based in the United States. The press specializes in Buddhist meditation and philosophy, as well as other topics from Buddhist perspectives including history, ethics, and governance. Its books are distributed worldwide and available in multiple languages. The bird mentioned in the company's name is said to be from a special place where beings can meet with favorable conditions to progress on their path to awakening.

Also by Shamar Rinpoche

BOUNDLESS AWAKENING
The Heart of Buddhist Meditation

THE PATH TO AWAKENING
How Buddhism's Seven Points of Mind Training Can Lead You to a Life of Enlightenment and Happiness

BOUNDLESS WISDOM
A Mahāmudrā Practice Manual

A GOLDEN SWAN IN TURBULENT WATERS
The Life and Times of the Tenth Karmapa Choying Dorje

THE KING OF PRAYERS
A Commentary on the Noble King of Prayers of Excellent Conduct

CREATING A TRANSPARENT DEMOCRACY
A New Model

Bringing Mind Training to Life

An Exploration of the 5th Shamarpa's
Concise Lojong Manual

A Book by Shamar Rinpoche

Introduction and glossary by Lama Jampa Thaye

Adapted for print by Pamela Gayle White

RABSEL
PUBLICATIONS

Table of Contents

Introduction

It was in June 2013 at Dhagpo Kagyu Ling in France that I requested that Shamar Rinpoche visit our English center, Kagyu Ling, the following year. My specific request was that he bestow the commentary on Géshé Chekawa's famous *Seven Points of Mind Training* (Lojong Dön Dünma) composed by his own eminent predecessor, the 5th Shamarpa Könchok Yenlak (1525–1583).

It seemed to me that it would be very auspicious for Dharma students to be able to receive the transmission of the 5th Shamarpa's work by the current fourteenth incarnation. Moreover, Rinpoche himself had long stressed the vital importance of the cycle of Dharma instructions connected with "mind training" (*lojong*). He had made it a central part of his efforts to bring an effective and lucid Dharma to the West.

Mind training, as a specific genre of teachings and practices within Tibetan Buddhism, originated in the early Kadam tradition in the eleventh century C.E. In fact, three main sets of Kadam teachings are usually distinguished: Classical Texts, Instructions, and Pith Instructions. The first of these consists of a number of works from India, such as Shantideva's famous *Introduction to the Bodhisattva Conduct*, the second consists of mind training, and the third contains the principal Tantric cycles of the tradition, such as *The Four Kadam Deities*.

It was the great Bengali master Atisha Dipamkara Shrijnana (979–1053) who brought the instructions for mind training to Tibet, although neither he nor the three teachers from whom he received these teachings appear to have actually referred to them as such. Indeed, despite the existence of specific texts composed by Atisha's masters Dharmarakshita, Maitriyogin, and Serlingpa (also known as Dharmakirti from Sumatra), which are now considered part of the mind training transmissions, Atisha himself only transmitted mind training as a set of oral instructions to Dromtönpa.

Consequently, while most of the lines in the famous *Seven Points of Mind Training* derive from Atisha, it was Chekawa Yéshé Dorjé (1102–1176) who actually arranged it in seven points. Géshé Chekawa's text became extraordinarily influential and inspired many commentaries, the first being that of his disciple, Sé Chilbupa (1121–1189). In subsequent centuries this would be followed by many more, including celebrated works by the Kadam/Sakya master Tokmé Zangpo (1295–1369) and the great Kagyu polymath Jamgön Kongtrül Lodrö Thayé (1811–1899).

Indeed, even now the flood of commentaries on the *Seven Points of Mind Training* continues unabated, with the recent publication of works by the 14th Shamar Rinpoche (1952–2014) himself as well as by Karma Thinley Rinpoche (1931–).

As regards the actual nature of mind training, it can best be described as a radical method of transforming ordinary mind, with its habits of self-clinging and self-cherishing, into the vast compassion and profound wisdom of *bodhicitta*, the thought of enlightenment itself. Although its roots lie in the Buddha's Mahayana sutras, one can find the core mind training theme of the need to "exchange oneself for others" delineated in the works of the Indian masters Shantideva, Nagarjuna and Asanga. Thus Shantideva states:

> "Whoever wishes to obtain enlightenment swiftly for both themselves and others should practice this supreme secret of exchanging oneself for others."

At the end of May 2014 Shamar Rinpoche spent three days with us at Kagyu Ling in Manchester. Over two hundred and fifty people attended his teachings on the Seven Points.

Although Shamar Könchok Yenlak's commentary seems to be stylistically and thematically closest to Tokmé Zangpo's earlier work, on this occasion Rinpoche wove the transmission of mahamudra into his teaching. Thus, for many who attended, it was an introduction to the nature of mind given by a master who was a holder of the lineage of mahamudra. In presenting the teachings in this way, Shamar Rinpoche made it clear that Kagyu Dharma is truly, as it is so often described, "the union of the two streams of Kadam and Mahamudra."

Lama Jampa Thaye
London, England
April 21, 2018

A Word about the Process

The last meeting I had with Mipham Chökyi Lodrö, the 14th Shamar Rinpoche, took place in Dordogne, France, late May 2014. We spoke about our translation projects, my plans, and some ideas for developing certain practices in the North and Latin American Bodhi Path centers. Rinpoche thanked me for my work within the mandala; he was particularly supportive that day. A few days later, he would give this, his penultimate teaching, at Kagyu Ling, Lama Jampa Thaye's center in Manchester, England.

I was especially keen on listening to the recordings because the teaching was based on a text I had translated: *A Concise Lojong Manual* by Könchok Yenlak, the 5th Shamarpa. This text became a booklet, first published by Marpa Kagyu Dharma Preservation Center in Kathmandu, then by Bird of Paradise Press in the US.

Listening to the Manchester teachings is a bitter-sweet experience—you *really* hear Shamar Rinpoche: his wisdom, humor, kindness, and dedication to helping all present get the point. He clearly appreciates the connection with Lama Jampa Thaye, the venue, and the opportunity to teach lojong in England. The little book by his predecessor seems tailor-made for a weekend lojong transmission, with plenty of space to go deep into ultimate bodhicitta. Shamar Rinpoche's clear emphasis on meditation and on folding the view of ultimate bodhicitta/emptiness into the practice of lojong is very much *him*. It's so familiar and enjoyable, and yet you know that right after this weekend he will give another teaching on the same subject using the same little book at Renchen Ulm in Germany, and it will be his last; he will transition in Renchen on June 11, 2014.

The challenge in putting together any book based on oral teachings is to make it readable while retaining the voice. I had worked closely with Shamar Rinpoche on translation projects; often we would play with terms and structures until the words and phrases felt right. I've taken a few liberties here, reworking paragraphs, moving sentences, erasing some repetitions, and, as seldom as possible, replacing words to improve accuracy and flow. I found it important to give readers a taste of the colorful and sometimes quirky language that Rinpoche would use to convey his insights in English.

The passages from *A Concise Lojong Manual* are presented in a different font. The first use of non-English terms is italicized. Many of these are presented in the glossary. A table at the end presents glossary terms in transliterated Sanskrit and Tibetan for interested readers.

Heartfelt thanks to Lama Jampa Thaye for supporting

the project and offering to write the introduction and glossary, and to Albena and the Dechen team for their timely and gracious help. A deep bow to Thea Howard for her knowledgeable transcription. Thanks to Brian Worthy and Stephanie Singer whose generosity gave me some space to work on this book. A loud shout out to Seth Watkins and Greg Mock for their expert and timely copyediting. Thanks also to Lodrö Rabsel Rinpoché for making the first edition of *A Concise Lojong Manual* a reality, and to Sabine Teuber for convincing Shamar Rinpoche that it was a handy little book for practitioners in the Bodhi Path and other centers to study and put into practice. And most of all, gratitude, always, to our tireless teachers, the beacons whose radiant wisdom illumines our paths.

Pamela Gayle White
Lexington, Virginia
September 3, 2018

Session 1

The practice of mind training, or *lojong* in Tibetan, is well known within the Mahayana tradition. In Tibet, lojong is combined with Vajrayana practice, especially in the Kagyu lineage. Gampopa, one of the main founders of the Kagyu school of Tibetan Buddhism, held two Buddhist lineages. One is the lineage that descended from Marpa through Milarepa, his guru. Another lineage is from Atisha to Dromtön and down to Gampopa, who wrote the *Jewel Ornament of Liberation* and other texts that mainly brought lojong and mahamudra together.

This commentary about lojong, the Seven Points of Mind Training, by the 5th Shamarpa is concise and handy. It has been translated into English by Pamela Gayle White, who is a translator for the Bodhi Path Buddhist Centers and is a teacher as well. I've also written a commentary on lojong called *The Path to Awakening.* So after you study this, you can go into *The Path to Awakening*. The arrangement of *The Path to Awakening* is a little different, but it will not be contradictory.

We have eight hours to go over this small book, so I will take advantage of the time and explain some *mahamudra* meditation instructions which correspond with absolute *bodhicitta*. Gampopa combined absolute bodhicitta practice and mahamudra. Generally, when the lojong teachings are explained, only the *madhyamaka* way is presented, but here I will explain the madhyamaka way as well as the mahamudra way.

I will read the commentary and then explain, starting after the history.[1]

> I take refuge in the perfect lama and in the most precious mind of awakening. The glorious Dharma Lord Atisha received these key instructions on training in developing bodhicitta, the mind of awakening, from Lama Serlingpa.
>
> Although there are many different teachings on the subject, this has been composed according to Spiritual Friend Chekawa's seven-point system.

"Spiritual friend" means spiritual master.

Lama Serlingpa—I think many of you already know about him—was one of the princes of Indonesia and a very great Buddhist master. He held both the lineage of

---

1 This book is the record of an oral commentary given by Mipham Chökyi Lodrö, the 14th Shamarpa, about a 16th century text called *A Concise Lojong Manual*, written by Könchok Yenlak, the 5th Shamarpa. *A Concise Lojong Manual* is a brief, accessible explanation of the lojong maxims transmitted by Atisha and organized by Chekawa Yéshé Dorjé into the famous seven points.
Here, the passages in a different font are taken directly from *A Concise Lojong Manual*.

the bodhisattva vow tradition that is descended from Manjushri through Nagarjuna, and the bodhisattva vow tradition that is descended from Maitreya through Asanga. In Atisha's time, the tradition of these "two lineages merged into one" had vanished from India. There are a number of historical records explaining why Atisha had to go to Indonesia to find it, but the one that is essential for us to know is that when Atisha was walking around the stupa in Bodh Gaya praying to the twenty-one Taras, Green Tara appeared and predicted that he should go to Indonesia to retrieve this combined lineage, then go to Tibet to spread Buddhism there.

This was a time when Tibetan kings commissioned and invited Buddhists into Tibet. Later, one of the kings of the royal lineage—Langdarma, the eighth, I think—was anti-Buddhist. The reason was that there were too many monks and they absorbed all the available food. King Langdarma thought that this was not good, so he organized economic and political reforms. The Buddhist monks were chased out and many of them had to leave the country. For about twelve years Tibet was free of Buddhism, which was not good for enlightenment but may have been good for the economy at that time.

Then the king was killed by a yogi of the Nyingma lineage, and two of the princes who were followers of Buddhism started to invite Buddhists back to Tibet. Atisha was the first official teacher who was invited to Tibet at that time. Before he went to Tibet, Atisha went to Indonesia and met Lama Serlingpa. Atisha received all of the lojong instructions as well as the bodhisattva vow lineages from Serlingpa, then he returned to India. Not long afterwards, he went to Tibet and spent the rest of his life there. The lojong lineage in Tibet is an unbroken transmission from that time until now.

Chekawa Yéshé Dorjé was a disciple of Géshé Sharawa, who was a close student of Potowa, a very famous Kadam lineage holder. When Chekawa heard [Potowa's disciple] Langri Thangpa's words explaining that self-clinging was the root of samsara and needed to be diminished, he was inspired by those words and went to see Sharawa to learn how to cut self-clinging. He spent thirteen years with his teacher Sharawa. At the end of this text he says that because of his intention he started practicing the methods that tame the ego and now his wish has been achieved, so "*Were I to die this instant, I would have no regrets.*"

This means that he began to reveal his lojong practice to his disciples at that time. He composed the seven points which include the whole lojong practice, and actually the whole of Buddhist practice. This structure using the seven points is very easy, technically, for disciples to follow.

The seven points are:

The preliminaries: presenting the practitioner's basic Dharma teachings.

The main practice: training in bodhicitta, awakening mind.

Transforming adverse circumstances into the path of awakening.

Explanations on incorporating the practice during one's lifetime.

Evaluating progress in mind training.

The mind training commitments.

The mind training guidelines.

The **first point: First, train in the preliminaries**.

> Consider the fact that although we now have a human
> body, it will be difficult to obtain one in the future.

First, we consider that it will be difficult to obtain a precious human life again. Of course there are many, many humans, but it is very, very rare for someone to have full opportunities to meet with the Dharma and put it into practice. This depends on your past deeds. If you have the good support of past deeds, then due to these past deeds, you'll use this life to practice the Dharma and this human life is indeed precious.

For instance, during Buddha's time, there was a shopkeeper who intended to practice Dharma and so he met with Kashyapa, I think, who was the Buddha's number one disciple. Kashyapa analyzed his qualities and told him, "No, I will not teach you. You will not be able to absorb my teachings because I don't see any karmic support for your practice." The shopkeeper then went to a few other disciples. All of them had the ability to see past merit, but since they were not buddhas, their understanding was limited. None of them found that this shopkeeper had the karmic support to practice the Dharma for enlightenment, so they all refused to teach him.

Finally, he managed to meet the Buddha. The Buddha said, "You *do* have the necessary karmic support. Many, many lifetimes ago you were on one of the planets where a buddha was teaching. There was a kind of stupa which was blessed by this buddha, and you were one of those black beetles which is always digging in the ground." It's a kind of beetle—I think it's the black one which has a big mouth and is very good at digging. [*audience: a dung beetle.*] Dung beetle, okay. There was a small flood which washed the earth, and the beetle hung on to some dry manure which was carried by the water. It passed through a stupa. That stupa was a wish-fulling stupa and because he passed through it he received its blessing! Due to that support he was qualified to practice! (*laughter*) He was a shopkeeper when he met the Buddha, then he gave up everything, followed the Buddha, and became an arhat. He was a very great vinaya master of his time.

So even as a human, if you are lacking the necessary karmic support, you will not be able to absorb the Dharma. Therefore, among the many, many humans, the one who has a precious human life is very rare. And you have it right now! I think many of you who are constantly coming to Dharma practice might have more karmic support than the blessing of the stupa for a little bug. You now have a precious human life, and you should use it.

> Consider that the time of death is uncertain; it may arrive all of a sudden.

Yes. In my lifetime I've had many friends who passed away. Many young friends passed away before old friends. Many old people are still living while many young people have already died. Since life is very fragile, the causes and circumstances of death can happen at any time.

And karma. All sentient beings have many kinds of karma—countless, in fact. In my book *The Path to Awakening*, I call it "pushy crowdy karma." I made that term up in English—I contributed it to English Buddhism! What does pushy crowdy karma mean? By "karma" we mean mental events which carry karma either through their connection to afflictions, or to expressions of meritorious mind like compassion. For as long as you have had self-clinging, you have had afflictions in the mind. During countless lifetimes you have accumulated karma through these afflictions. All the karma has been and will be stored in the consciousness.

Like in dreams. You have a lot of dreams that are caused by weak karmic thoughts, by a mind which does not have strong karmic power and therefore it produces short dreams. All the consciousnesses are backed by the nature of the ground consciousness. On the surface, on the screen of the mind, all kinds of illusions can rise up and connect to the different kinds of karma. So while you are sleeping, your mind goes back to the ground consciousness, and during that time the small aspects of mind which carry some karma create dreams. As far as our experience is concerned, what we see and experience now during the daytime, what we experience in a dream, and what we experience in the bardo are all of the same nature: they are caused by karma. Here karma refers to the mental events that produce different illusions.

Having a human life in this world is also our illusion; it may be caused by good karma or mixed karma or very bad karma. Different individuals experience life differently in connection with their past karma. It's very powerful to take the refuge vow and the bodhisattva vow; they carry a lot of merit that can prevent bad karmas from ripening. Bad karmas which have not yet ripened and may disturb your life can already be prevented by strong positive deeds such as bodhisattva vows. The opportunity is there.

Right now you have met with the Dharma and received the blessings of the refuge vow and bodhisattva vow, so the influence of negative karma is already weakened. Sometimes, unfortunately, negative karma can disturb your life. Anything can happen. Therefore, you should not be overconfident about the length of your life. You must use the opportunity that you have right now for enlightenment.

As I said, in the bardo, "pushy crowdy karma" refers to all the karmas that are ready to ripen. In the bardo, the conditions for karma to ripen are present. Many, many karmas are ready to ripen; one pushes past the others, and this strongest one determines what will happen. Like for King Ashoka, who in his early life was very evil, and then later he became very great and sponsored many, many Buddhist monuments in the world. He was very generous and was a great sponsor of the Buddhadharma. At the end of his life, the nurse who was fanning him hit him on the head with the fan. Ashoka was so upset and angry that it caused his sudden death.

Because of that strong karma due to anger, in the bardo he entered the womb of a python. He became a snake for a while. His master, an arhat, had to go to the snake and shout, calling Ashoka's name loudly. Then the snake remembered his blessings and his past and understood that he was mistakenly in the form of a snake. He deliberately stopped eating and died so he could discontinue being in a lower realm as a snake.

Karma is so powerful! During our time in the bardo, all of our karmas are ready to ripen, so circumstances are very important. Merit is the only thing that can help, and among all forms of merit, bodhicitta is the most powerful. As Shantideva says, if you can hold on to a small log while being carried by a strong flood, you'll have a chance of being saved. The bodhisattva vow is a very powerful meritorious action that can save you from samsara: it can carry you from the flood. Among all practices, the bodhisattva vow and the practice of bodhicitta generate the strongest positive karma.

| Consider that all cyclic existence entails suffering. |

We all experience this actually. This physical form is very fragile and we experience all kinds of sickness. Mentally, we experience all kinds of depression and anxiety. Yes, sometimes you are happy, but it's not reliable. It can easily change and you will suffer. The "suffering of change" that we experience after happiness has ended is unbearable, but there are other kinds of suffering that are experienced constantly. Of course, the illusion [that we call life] is full of causes and conditions. For example, the "suffering of suffering" is constant suffering, like being in the lower realms.

In this life as a human, you will also experience a lot of "subtle suffering." Subtle suffering is like a pain in the stream of the mind. It's "subtle" because, as humans, we don't recognize it. It means that there is no peace in the stream of the mind, and because there's no peace, we don't experience ultimate happiness. The subtle suffering of the stream of mind continues forever. It has been like this since beginningless time and it will continue. Only the realization of mind's nature can save you entirely from subtle suffering. Otherwise it will continue and that's how it is for all living beings who dwell in samsara. Cyclic existence, or samsara, means up and down, up and down, up and down, constantly.

Subtle suffering is connected to self-clinging and is based on the dualistic process of the mind. As long as mind is trapped in a dualistic perception of subject and object, it has to make contact with objects through different sense faculties. If mind is perceived to be one thing and mind's object as another, then you crave the object. That habit is deeply rooted in the stream of the mind; therefore mind has no peace. We all experience this.

No peace in the mind is the cause of all forms of suffering. The suffering of suffering—as experienced constantly in the hell realms—and the suffering of change are superficial forms of suffering. The origin of all forms of suffering is subtle suffering, and once you realize mind's true nature, it will vanish.

Consider that suffering originates in non-virtue, and happiness originates in goodness.

There are many kinds of happiness, such as the happiness of heavenly life. In human societies as well, some people are very happy and you can see that everything is okay for them. However, it is not permanent: old age and death are there. Sickness is there. People's happiness results from meritorious actions. But still, as long as the habit of self-clinging is present, there will be afflictions in the depths of the mind and there can be no permanent refuge from the problems and sufferings of samsara.

Non-virtue comes from ego, from self-clinging. Anything you say or do that is influenced by the afflictions of self-clinging will be negative. Negative actions will give negative results—this is easy to understand. Happiness is caused by virtue, by meritorious actions, but if the meritorious actions don't root out ego and self-clinging, the resulting happiness won't be totally reliable. There will be some good results, but they will come to an end. The only virtue you can truly rely on is ultimate virtue: the realization of ultimate bodhicitta.

For the meditation of ultimate bodhicitta, you first

have to accomplish *shiné* meditation. Without the support of shiné, you can never develop ultimate bodhicitta. In Könchok Yenlak's commentary, taking the refuge and bodhisattva vows and shiné practice are part of the second point. In my book, *The Path to Awakening*, they are part of the first point: preliminary practices.

> The **second point, the main practice**, is training in developing both aspects of awakening mind: ultimate bodhicitta and conventional bodhicitta.
>
> The preparation phase of the former, [ultimate bodhicitta,] takes place before the lama and the three jewels, whether materially present or visualized. Recite the "Manam" refuge until the mind has been transformed . . .

In this Tibetan prayer *ma* means "mother" and *nam* means "sky." All living beings under the sky are my mother; all sentient beings under the sky, including myself, take refuge in the Buddha, the Dharma, and the Sangha. We take refuge in the guru, the lama, who is not separate from *dharmakaya*, *sambhogakaya*, and *nirmanakaya*. You'll find this prayer in the Kagyu four foundations practice. Otherwise, of course, you can take refuge in the Buddha, Dharma, and Sangha and then take the bodhisattva vow

> . . . then offer a seven-branch prayer and develop bodhicitta thus:

The seven-branch prayer was very wisely organized by the masters of the past. All the meritorious practices that are needed in order to develop enlightenment are present in the seven-branch practice.

In the [more extensive] "Samantabhadra Wishing Prayer," [which begins with a seven-branch prayer,] you visualize the pure land of Buddha Amitabha on each and every one of the atoms in the universe. You can visualize this instantly, like when a mirror is facing a valley and you can see the whole valley appearing in the mirror. In addition to Buddha Amitabha's pure land, there are many other pure lands that are manifested by buddhas. Try to visualize one on top of each of the atoms of the universe.

Then imagine that in every one of the buddha realms that you've visualized on each of the atoms, you are present as a volunteer leading sentient beings. Imagine that you have managed to bring all sentient beings to that pure land. In each of these pure realms you are the one who is these sentient beings' sponsor; you are the one who requested that the buddhas come teach them. All living beings are in precious human form and all are participating in the pure realm. They see and meet the buddhas, and because of your arrangements they all receive the precious teachings and achieve realization and the buddha *bhumis*.

In the [shorter] seven-branch practice as well, first you should think that each atom carries a buddha realm. In that realm you are the one who is leading all beings in making prostrations to the buddhas in order to accumulate the merit power to liberate all sentient beings. Each being is able to manifest splendid offerings to the buddhas, and in order to be free from karmic obscurations they are all engaged in precious practices such as confession, like Dorjé Sempa practice. They all become free from the karma of their bad deeds. Because you are leading, and all the sentient beings in the buddha realms are following your practice, you rejoice in the merit of all buddhas, bodhisattvas, arhats, and pratyekabuddhas.

Recently, I met a scientist in Washington DC who told me that scientists had focused their telescope on the darkest part of the sky for twenty-four hours and they found one billion milky galaxies! One billion! As the Buddha taught in the Samantabhadra practice, realms are like that. It is not like one being is pushing the other—it's like *Alice in Wonderland*: everything is clearly there.

They say that in some universes, even though buddhas appear, they stay just one week after becoming enlightened and then leave because sentient beings' accumulation of meritorious karma is lacking. Somebody has to *ask* a buddha to teach. Here you are manifesting yourself in every realm where there are buddhas, and you take the initiative to request that the buddhas give teachings in order to liberate sentient beings. Also, you are the one who leads sentient beings in requesting that the buddhas live forever.

The last verse is dedicating our merit for sentient beings. This means that we are totally free from practicing for any personal reasons. Like with the blessing that saved the black beetle, whatever merit we may have accumulated should work for sentient beings. So we dedicate. The masters very wisely organized a short but great seven-branch practice that you too can accomplish.

> *Until the heart of awakening has become manifest, I take refuge in the buddhas. Likewise, I take refuge in the Dharma and the assembly of bodhisattvas.*
>
> *Just as the sugatas of the past cultivated awakening mind and progressively trained as bodhisattvas, stage by stage, for the sake of beings, I too will foster awaken-*

ing mind and train just as they did, stage by stage.

You all have received the bodhisattva vow. The bodhisattva vow has two aspects. One is aspiration. The bodhisattva aspiration is like an intention, a willingness to have the same genuine attitude of bodhicitta that past buddhas and bodhisattvas had. The second aspect is that you engage totally in bodhisattva practice, the same activities that past bodhisattvas practiced in order to accomplish buddhahood. *Paramita* practice is the path of the bodhisattva; there are six paramitas or ten paramitas. *Paramita* means the accomplishment of bodhisattva activity. With the ten paramita list, the sixth paramita—the paramita of wisdom or intelligence—is subdivided into qualities such as the practice of wishes or aspirations, as in Samantabhadra's wishing practice. Another is power: the bodhisattvas' power is expanded to help sentient beings.

There's an example of the paramita of skillful means or methods where Maitreya manifested in order to liberate living beings whose vision was very, very limited and humans were very small—their world had become very small—because they lacked merit. Maitreya Buddha went there; he was much taller than others and beautiful looking. The small humans asked, "Why are you good looking and bigger than the rest of us?" He answered, "Because I practice the ten virtues." "What are the ten virtues?" Then Maitreya taught. So these are skillful means where the power of method is spontaneously implemented according to sentient beings' fortune and circumstances.

Wishing, or aspirations, is also like Buddha Amitabha's activity. He accomplished the wish that he had dedicated for sentient beings: the moment he became a buddha, the pure land of Buddha Amitabha manifested.

The paramita of power refers to expanding the blessings of the bodhisattvas. For instance, thanks to the power of the stupa, the beetle eventually became an arhat. And finally, the paramita of wisdom: the six paramitas plus wishes, methods, power, and wisdom. Wishes, methods, power, and wisdom are each connected to one of the bhumis—the seventh, eighth, ninth, and tenth bhumis. Wisdom is the tenth bhumi. When you have accomplished and developed the full wisdom of the buddhas and bodhisattvas—*completely* accomplished, *completely* developed—then you are a buddha.

> With this, practice refuge and bodhicitta, invoke the deities and lamas, and offer an extensive seven-branch prayer. Straighten your physical posture and breathe serenely in and out twenty-one times—no more, no less. This is how one becomes a suitable vessel for meditative stability.

Here, deities and lamas are included, which, according to Vajrayana, is okay. *Breathe serenely in and out twenty-one times—no more, no less.* This "no more, no less" is a little uncomfortable for me; "serenely" is good. Here, I think the translator might easily have misunderstood the Tibetan term, "no more, no less." That's because when you're counting twenty-one times, you might miscount. It can happen. It means that your mind is distracted; it isn't concentrated properly on the breath. Why do you concentrate on the breath? Superficially you might say that it's easier for you, because the breath is always with you.

According to Buddhist medical biology, the breath is very important. Breathing gently and concentrating on the breath is additionally very, very effective for increasing peace of mind. Most of the time, the movement of the mind and your physical breath go together; they are simultaneous. When you concentrate on your breath, all the breath in the subtle channels gathers into one area of the body and creates more physical tranquility. When the physical body experiences tranquility, that will serve your mind as well. Of course, this is not a contaminated tranquility, like when you take hallucinogenic drugs. It's a totally uncontaminated tranquility; when you are able to concentrate on your breath as you breathe gently out-in, out-in, it is a comfort, a balance, which is very energetic.

As beginners, you can count one, exhale, two, inhale. Next, according to my experience, it is very effective to exhale, inhale, one, and count to twenty-one breathing cycles in that way. By counting twenty-one times and focusing on the breath, the beginner's mind can easily concentrate very well.

Mind is like a wild horse, so you have to tame it first and make it obedient. Meditators already experience this, but those of you who have never meditated will realize that mind is very wild, like a wild horse, and not easy to control. When you ride a wild horse, it jumps at everything; it's very disobedient in the beginning. But once you have trained it the right way, suddenly it becomes very relaxed and obeys whatever you order it to do. In the beginning, you have to be strong enough to face that; with patience you can easily control it. The method is to concentrate on the breath, exhale, inhale, exhale, inhale.

In order to avoid becoming drowsy or falling asleep, you can visualize a bright color, like white. Imagine that your breath appears as a beam of light, and as you exhale it goes this way [moves hand down from nostrils towards the floor]. Inhale the beam of light back towards the lungs or inside your body, then exhale and it goes out like that independently [and unattached to the body]. Then it comes back. Do you understand? Independently means one tip is almost touching the ground and the other end is here [just inside the nostrils], almost coming out. On the inhale it can go up [towards the brain] and then down [to the lungs or belly], like a hook. One end is in the lungs or the belly, or wherever you like, and the other end is [just outside the nostrils]. No need to blow your nose. Okay? In some instructions the beam [is like an arc when you exhale], but in a sutra it says that it's [straight].

So you count twenty-one times, and then take a short break. In general, when you meditate it is fine to start over again, but here it says only twenty-one breath cycles at the beginning of the practice to prepare your mind.

Generally, you train your mind with shiné practice. Among shiné techniques, the most effective method to pacify your mind is to practice using the breath. By counting the breath cycles and visualizing breath as a beam of light, your mind will become clear. Focusing on the movement of the breath and on counting is one of the most effective ways to reduce thoughts and pacify the mind.

When you practice shiné, after twenty-one times you can have a short break and then start again. Quickly your mind will get used to it. You can choose your objective. For example, when it becomes easier, clearly easier, then you can extend the counting up to fifty times. Then when it becomes easy for you to do fifty times, you can extend up to a hundred times. Then from a hundred times you can extend up to a thousand times. When you can do one thousand times comfortably and easily, you will have maximum progress. You will experience such enormous peace in the mind that it will captivate you. You will like it! At that time, the teacher should warn you, discourage you from clinging to the peace or craving it. If you cling to it, the comfort in the mind will change into something else.

To pacify the mind, counting breath cycles is the best method. Here awareness is very, very important. When you concentrate on your breath and count, you have to be very conscious about whether awareness is there or not. If you are fully aware of what is happening in the mindstream, of where the mind is focused, then when any disturbing thoughts arise, you will recognize that. The moment you recognize it, you can bring the focus back to the point. That is awareness.

With dullness, for a long time you won't realize that your mind is thinking about something else. That is the distraction of dullness, which can develop into a very bad habit. You have to be very serious about correcting it. Agitation is easier to notice and control, but the distraction of dullness is nearly invisible, unnoticeable. It is very difficult to control. This is why you should try to recognize the distraction of dullness in the beginning and bring the mind back.

Sometimes dullness can develop if your eyes are not correctly oriented. Your eyes should look gently beyond the slope of the nose at this [downward] angle. When you sit like this and keep your eyes at this angle, you will see part of the nose—but that doesn't mean that you should *try* to look at the tip of the nose. Keeping your eyes positioned at the right level will help you not fall into dullness.

Maintain awareness. Keep your spine straight. The right hand rests on the palm of the left hand and the elbows are squeezed against your body. If you are on a cushion with your legs crossed, then your hands are supported by your lap. The neck is bent down a bit. Raise the shoulders like an eagle's wings. Keep the stomach in. If you push the breath down in the belly a little and hold it in the abdomen below the navel, that's fine. This is a good position. It is not that you are trying to hold the breath in the stomach like yoga, but that you are gently keeping the stomach in. Make yourself comfortable. It's very important to be comfortable. If you lean to the right or left, that will create certain thoughts, a kind of strong disturbance, in the mind. So you should keep very straight and balanced. Is it clear?

Beginners should not eat food that is too rich in the afternoon. Not so much cheese—like the French—or fatty foods—like a giant steak. Some people eat a giant steak in the evening and it's very heavy. Having a light stomach, eating light food is very, very helpful for meditation. One could skip dinner, of course, which is very, very good, but people who have to work cannot do that, so light food, okay? Instead of eating heavy food in the evening, you can switch heavy food to the morning and light food in the evening; this will help very much for meditation.

> The second phase [of training in ultimate bodhicitta] is the main one.

To develop shiné means developing concentration. Usually, no one has concentration in the mind; no one naturally has it most of the time unless one is hibernating. [*laughter*] Hibernating isn't sleeping, is it? Otherwise there is no peace in the mind, no concentration. Now, the way how you cut out the root of ego, of self-clinging, is through meditation: advanced meditation, like maha-mudra meditation, madhyamaka meditation. But right now, your mind cannot do those practices because you have no concentration power. To develop concentration power and free the mind from too much thinking, you have to train the mind to focus on one point. Then, nat-urally, there are methods that can be used as antidotes.

Focus on one object and train your mind to concen-trate on it spontaneously. "Training" means making an effort, but it has to be an effort with the right methods. The *shamatha* or shiné meditations are the methods that train your mind to be able to concentrate. I'm tell-ing you: get used to it. When you can concentrate spon-taneously, that means that your mind is well trained. *Then* you can do the more advanced meditations that make it possible to completely root out the problems of the mind.

Concentrating on the breath is one method for train-ing the mind. Counting the cycles of exhale and inhale is one of the very, very effective methods to train your mind to be able to concentrate. Is it clear?

> **Consider all phenomena as dreams**.
> Consider that they are nothing more than the mind's confused projections and do not exist outside of it.

Logically, you can understand that all phenomena are like dreams, but you will not *experience* them as dreams. You will only experience all phenomena to be like dreams when your meditation is fully matured, fully developed. But in order to subdue wrong views about phenomena, it is very important to understand how all phenomena are like a mirage; they're not really existing. Therefore, the big subjects of *yogachara* and madhyamaka were developed in order to logically prove that all phenomena are like a mirage. They are not real.

I say, "Alice in Wonderland." While Alice was sleeping, she had a long dream. Then she wrote the dream down, and it became a big book. But she could have had that dream within five minutes of sleeping. According to our time it was five minutes or maybe fifteen minutes sleeping, but when the whole dream was written down it became a book. We can all have similar dreams even if we only sleep for a short while. The dream really exists for you while you are dreaming, doesn't it? You can analyze it: you sleep for five minutes and have a dream, and then you wake up and write it down, and it is thirty minutes long! How? You slept for five minutes. There wasn't enough time for you to have that dream that took you thirty minutes to write. So how did it happen?

All phenomena exist in your mind only; they're not really there. Take sounds: if there is no ear, how can there be sound independently? Sound depends on the ear! Sound cannot listen by itself. Forms: what you see— colors, shapes—everything depends upon the eyes of living beings. Feeling: what we feel, cold, hot, everything depends upon the sense of feeling of living beings. Up, down, right, left, back, front all of them entirely depend on the minds of living beings! How can right or left exist by themselves? If they existed by themselves, then right would be there without left. It cannot be there! As long as you have a mind, you have up and down, right and left. All are within the mind—they cannot exist externally, independently. All from mind. All phenomena are dreams like that.

Even scientists say something like that nowadays.

They understand some part of it; not everything, but some part. The smallest of atoms are supposed to be the root of creating this great big giant Earth, but the smallest atoms have no sides, so the atom is a mirage, like zero.

One very stubborn German scientist maintains that zero exists. I told him that zero cannot exist because we are not zeros, and without us how can zero itself exist? He could not understand my logic because he was so stubborn about it. But I do have hope that scientists will slowly understand.

> **Examine the unborn nature of awareness.**
> Consider that mind is also free of beginning, cessation, and dwelling.
> **The remedy too liberates itself naturally.**

There's a very famous saying from Shantideva that all the Buddhist masters quote: "Having understood that disturbing emotions are completely overcome by insight endowed with calm-abiding, first of all I should seek calm-abiding." That's the way to fully develop enlightenment.

It means that mind liberates itself naturally. For it to liberate itself naturally, of course you have to do the practice, constantly, with the right methods, as described here:

> Look at the very mind of that person who is watching and meditating: it too is free of beginning, cessation, and dwelling. Colorless and formless, it does not reside anywhere in or out of the body; it has no innate nature. Therefore, settle in a thought-free state without any intellectual grasping whatsoever.

The great meditators all go into this meditation, and then, when they realize that mind is free of shape, color, size, and location, they are so inspired by the experience that they start singing songs. "I have no words to explain it!" they say. "I have no illustration to show to people, but I have experienced it!" Milarepa was singing songs alone all the time. He was fully enjoying without any audience; he did not expect an audience.

When you go into the insight view of the nature of mind, you realize that every thought is unborn: it has no beginning and no end because the present thought doesn't carry any solidness. Like if you have a dream about a horse, the horse has no beginning, no cessation. Every thought carries the same nature: there's no beginning, no cessation, nothing is there, and you can realize this.

I will try to show you how I watch my mind. Maybe you can judge whether I am in it or not by the expression on my face, okay? [*laughter*] I will try and then you also can try afterward, or maybe at the same time. [*pause*] I cannot do it because I'm laughing now. [*loud laughter*] The present mind is the mind that you look at. Past mind is already gone, but you don't have to look for where it has gone. The present mind: watch the present mind. [*brief meditation*] Can you make it out? Can you make out that I am watching my present mind, roughly? I am not looking at this room, okay? I am looking at mind. [*more meditation time*] I could ignore all of you easily. [*laughter*]

If you can persist in this way, then the nature of mind will be more and more clear to you. Although my eyes are open, I am not looking at the colors here. I'm not thinking about all of you watching me. I've managed to hold my mind and not follow what I'm thinking about or notice that I am preparing to think of something else. I'm just casually watching my present mind, and I can sit in this quite comfortably. [*more meditation*]

Okay, thank you. We'll stop here.

Session 2

How should we understand *the unborn nature of mind?*
Analytically, *unborn* means no beginning, no end. The
present mind has no shape, no color, no size, but it is in
our experience. It is not like a coma. It is mind: we are
fully aware. Yes, we explain it, but the explanation is not
something that you have to *apply*. You have to directly
experience it. No need to think that mind is shapeless,
sizeless, colorless—you don't have to try to think in this
way. But when you can recognize the present moment
of mind and look into it, look at it with your mind, then
you will experience that it *is* mind. Freshly, you are aware
of it, but you cannot say that it singularly exists within
this or that. When a thought appears you don't have to
try to stop it—you use every thought to examine it.

This is basic mahamudra. As the practice develops
there are a lot of different experiences in keeping with
one's level of realization. Accordingly, the masters give

labels such as "one-pointed," "simplicity," "one taste," and "beyond meditation." "One-pointed" means you are in it, as I explained. [The levels of] this process are classified as small, medium, and high.

Right now it is the time for learning and you can't imagine these states. But when you reach "simplicity," for example, you will realize what it is. When you can maintain one-pointedness very well and have reached the highest level of one-pointed meditation, then you will experience that mind is totally free and spacious. No obstructions. Simplicity is the experience of the non-obstruction of mind.

The simplicity experience will lead you, again, through small, medium, and high, and then to "one taste." Naturally, human language is limited when trying to explain anything about meditation levels, because one has to experience them. But once you've had the experience, these terms take on a very different meaning.

"One taste" is just a metaphor. It means that you will be able to implement the experience you've had on each one of your thoughts. There's no good and no bad: you are totally free from that. You remain in one taste: neither good nor bad, and nothing there to judge. Great practitioners sometimes go into a crowd to test their minds and to see whether they can maintain their one taste experience or not.

I saw a yogi sleeping in the middle of the platform of the New Delhi train station. He pretended that he was sleeping, but he was not really sleeping. He wanted people to step on him and kick him. In mahamudra meditation, good meditators go into public areas to see whether they have discriminating thoughts or not, like "Oh, this is good, that is bad." Or "I'm happy when somebody treats me nicely" or "Wow, that person kicked me and treated me like I'm not human." If they do have those thoughts, they use them and implement the view on them. They can achieve a lot in this short-cut way when they go into a crowd like that. Of course, good teachers will only suggest going into this kind of extreme practice when practitioners are ready. Otherwise they will not encourage them to do that.

When you have a lot of confidence in the experience, this will lead to small, medium, and high, and then to "beyond meditation." At that point, you don't have to force your mind to go into meditation; you can go into meditation spontaneously. The experience is maintained consistently, even when you are working and talking with people. When you reach that consistency, it's already a very, very high level. "Beyond meditation" also has small, medium, and high.

According to the *Prajnaparamita Sutra*, the *siddhis*, or realizations, of "one-pointedness" and "simplicity" correspond with the first through sixth bhumis. Then the sixth to the tenth bhumis correspond with the siddhis of "simplicity" and "one taste." "Beyond meditation" is the level of enlightenment. I tell you this just for the idea, for the sake of comparison. In the sutras, there are ten bhumis. In mahamudra there are the Four Yogas [of one-pointedness, simplicity, one taste, and beyond meditation] which are then subdivided into small, medium, and high, so there are twelve. The twelve stages and ten bhumis are different ways of explaining the stages of meditative realization, but the meaning is the same.

All of these meditations can be developed from one ground: *Examine the unborn nature of awareness.* Initially, it is not easy, but once you can catch it, you can continue; you can maintain the experience and it will grow by itself. It is like when you weld two pieces of iron together, sparks will fly. Some sparks disappear the moment they fly and some almost touch the ground and then disappear. When you have experienced the unborn nature of mind, you can apply that experience to every moment of mind, and mind naturally liberates itself.

The moment you implement this examination, mind will be released from the trap of subject and object: dualism, dualistic mind, dual view. Usually your experience is dualistic: yourself and others. Now it will flow into one.

Clarity is the characteristic of a mind that is totally free from any shapes, sizes, or colors, and is not connected to any thoughts or whatever. Mind's nature is emptiness; we call it empty. Emptiness means that it is free from anything that you can think exists. The nature of mind is free from all existence. Its character is very clear.

Mind has its own experience. Mind does not need someone else to look at it—it is experienced by itself. And it is spacious: countless thoughts can arise from it, and contrarily, all kinds of limitless peace can be developed within mind. The state of non-dualism can develop within mind. We can also use the usual term, which is wisdom. In other words, limitless wisdom can grow within mind. Mind is resourceful: everything can happen within it.

[As for how to settle, it is said that:]

The essence of the path is to settle in the nature of *alaya*, the ground of all experience.

This is similar to what I've already explained. It means that you will not say, "Oh, this is the remedy which I've used to solve a certain problem. Now the problem is solved." No, there's nothing like that. The experience that you apply to every thought will work effectively, and the remedy will no longer exist separately. Your mind will go into its nature—the ground—spontaneously. *Alaya* is a Sanskrit term for ground, like space: the ground of all experience.

Can you tell me, how do you understand this? If anyone has doubts, or maybe if you do have a good understanding of it, it would be helpful if someone would tell me. Is it clear or not? Does your present mind exist as a separate entity or not? Or does a *quantity* of your mind exist—like money, rich people's money? Maybe you are craving for that, yeah, so then "quantity of mind." You can count from one to millions; you can have that many thoughts. But as far as the *nature* of mind is concerned, it is one. So no money and yes money: same. When you're craving it, you can count and accumulate one million thoughts, yeah? [*laughs*] Okay?

> The third phase [of training in ultimate bodhicitta] is the post-meditation practice.
>
> **Between sessions, be someone who is in tune with illusion.**

Here, after you have had a good experience of it, you will not force your mind, but you will clearly understand that everything is like a mirage. You will clearly experience it. If you read the songs of Milarepa, he explains a lot about his experience of understanding everything to be like a mirage.

Analytically, you can examine every phenomenon and you will conclude that nothing is real. Like I told you this morning, as with right/left, up/down: all are made up by mind. One simply cannot exist independently.

You can apply that view to daily things in order to prevent the craving and attachment which might disturb your meditation. Attachment here is like grasping. You are grasping so strongly that you are always creating problems. Implement this view to subdue the degree of grasping by thinking that all is illusion.

> Once you have realized that all phenomena are inherently non-existent and illusion-like, be without any yearnings regarding food, clothing, home, friends, enemies, and so on.

This is how ultimate bodhicitta is developed, how you do the practice of ultimate bodhicitta.

> The second aspect [of the second main point, training in bodhicitta, awakening mind] is training in relative bodhicitta during meditation and afterwards.
>
> As for the former, **practice sending and taking alternately.**

This is general, a very general instruction on how to develop compassion towards sentient beings. In all the Buddha's doctrines it says,

> Love all living beings as your mother and meditate with potent compassion on the suffering they now experience. Imagine that whatever harms these mothers—all torments of suffering and emotions—enters your heart. Wish fervently for the joy of having this actually happen. What can relieve our mothers' distress? They are helped by happiness and virtue. Therefore, we meditate that as all of our joy and goodness is absorbed by our mothers, they instantly become happy, all conditions for accomplishing Dharma practice are complete, and they are able to attain enlightenment.

This is general: you should always be aware of others' minds. If you are concerned about others' minds and what they want, then when someone is disappointed, you should be aware of that disappointment and what kind of feeling it is. When someone is very happy, ask yourself what *you* feel. Do you need happiness? What kind of happiness do you need? What kinds of suffering in the mind, like disappointments, don't you need? If someone else experiences them, then you will realize, "It was terrible for me, so I don't want others to experience it."

Think of others. If you think about others' feelings, then there is no way that you will not have compassion, unless you are really evil, in a trance, or possessed. You will have compassion when you are concerned about others' minds. If you think of all others as your mother, very good. Even if you don't, if you're concerned about their feelings and their suffering, then surely you will have genuine compassion. Try to think, "All living beings need happiness, and all living beings do not need suffering."

Someone who does not have a good knowledge of mind cannot feel others' sufferings. Therefore, many, many people in the world think humans have feelings, of course, and also dogs and horses have feelings. But then when they want something to eat, like lobsters and crabs, they don't think that they have feelings. They even play with lobsters by dipping them in hot water while the lobster is screaming. They can play like this because they don't know that lobsters have feelings—they're not in the habit of thinking of them like dogs or horses. I myself have seen cooks dip shellfish in hot water little by little because they like to hear the "music." The lobster is actually screaming but they think it is a kind of natural music. Or they put red wine on live shrimp on a plate and the shrimp cannot bear the pain and jump around—the cooks think it is a natural dance, just for fun. These animals are not domestic animals like dogs and horses, so the cooks don't treat them very well because of their ignorance. It is not really that they are mean. They don't know mind, and because they don't know mind, they don't know others' feelings.

It is very precious knowledge to know what living beings are. Other living beings have the same mind, the same feelings that you have. When you are concerned about others' feelings then naturally you will have compassion. Try to develop these good thoughts. Actually world peace also depends on your mind, and on this precious knowledge about the minds of living beings. All the crazy religions—like killing others in the name of one's deities—are developed from not knowing. They don't know. That's why they do it.

Train your mind through this practice to develop true compassion. When your intention is for others to have true happiness, that's love. When you feel concern for the suffering of others, that's compassion. As you dislike suffering and like love, you should wish the same for others. So here now is a great remedy, a way to accumulate limitless merit through bodhicitta in order to achieve nirmanakaya and sambhogakaya.

Buddha's enlightenment is classified in terms of the three kayas: nirmanakaya, sambhogakaya, and dharmakaya. Dharmakaya is the realization of enlightenment. Sambhogakaya and nirmanakaya are the natural manifestation of that realization in order to help and liberate other sentient beings. The supreme example is Buddha Shakyamuni, who came to our world as a great teacher and managed to dedicate all of his precious realization for humans so that many, many, many humans would achieve buddhahood as well. We continue to follow the Buddha's teachings because the wishes that the realized ones made for sentient beings are still being accomplished.

For a wish to be the cause that produces such precious help for sentient beings depends on genuine merit, without attachment. Any merit to which you are attached is limited. It doesn't carry limitless power because attachment is contamination. But the merit that results from any compassion or help that you generate towards sentient beings by knowing that everything is like a dream—so you have no attachment—will grow limitlessly because the quality of the merit matches the illusion of sentient beings.

When sentient beings have problems, you need a remedy to solve their problems, and the remedy manifests accordingly. When they need something good, you will also have the cause that will allow you to produce the good thing that sentient beings need. Whatever they need is an illusion, and the cause for that illusion is there too. One is within the other, and therefore it is the antidote. Compassion.

Here I'm explaining more technically. Certain forms of merit solve others' problems as well as *your* problems. The remedy and the problem have to match. Therefore, sentient beings naturally need a physical form [to help them solve their problems]. The mind is clinging to a self as "me," so you need to identify with "my" form. The kind of form you will have depends on the cause within your mind. Mostly, afflictions arise because you have self-clinging, so "I" need something.

If a problem is created by afflictions, any movement of mind which counters the afflictions will produce a positive result, right? For example, instead of having the form of a scorpion, you have beautiful butterflies. Even among insects it goes like that, yah?

If you have a form that is fully conditioned by the right faculties, then you can use your human form for good reasons. When our eyes and ears are fully conditioned by the right faculties, we can see and communicate. Accordingly, help can be generated for others. That definitely depends upon good causes. Good causes can be accumulated only out of compassion and lovingkindness and selflessness.

So this is a powerful training: you are adopting *tonglen*. The practice focusing on realizing the unborn nature of mind goes first and then you go into tonglen practice: you combine them together. And the result will be dharmakaya, sambhogakaya, and nirmanakaya, combined together.

The bodhisattva's compassion practice that is free from attachment is unlimited—not like the lady who went to Africa to save the gorillas. She did have compassion, but so much emotion was involved. Her compassion produced some good results, but the results were limited because of her attachment. Here, for tonglen practice, you need to be free from attachment. When you are concerned about others' suffering, this needs to be free from attachment. When you make the wish that others have happiness, this needs to be free from attachment. That's why you begin with the unborn nature of mind practice, and after that you combine it with tonglen practice. Then your practice will develop the three kayas: dharmakaya, sambhogakaya, and nirmanakaya.

Place these two on the breath.

[Meditate that when you breathe in, the negativities and pain of beings dissolve into you; when you breathe out, your happiness and virtue are absorbed by beings.]

To do this practice, again use your breath. Exhale all the great merit accumulated through your bodhisattva practice—such as taking the bodhisattva vows—for sentient beings, like light rays, instantly. For instance, all the big and small ponds in the world can have a simultaneous reflection of the sun when the sun is rising in the sky. It's the same: your help is received by all sentient beings at the same time when you exhale. Inhale, and instantly all of the problems and the roots of the problems of all sentient beings, the suffering and the cause of the suffering are removed. Sentient beings are relieved of all of this as it is absorbed by you. Do it this way many, many, many times.

Tonglen is a collection of so many important practices—compassion, non-attachment, concentration. Freedom from attachment means that everything is like a mirage. Nothing exists really; nothing exists independently. That's why I use the dream of Alice in Wonderland—she could dream all kinds of things. The rabbit is playing the guitar and the caterpillar is manifesting nirmanakaya!

Anything can happen within the mind, so here, as you exhale, you generate help for sentient beings without attachment and it can happen—you can engage in their scenarios. Like Buddha Shakyamuni who came as a buddha in human form, engaged in our human experience, and helped us.

When you inhale, absorb and remove all sentient beings' suffering and then exhale. Combine the practice:

inhale, exhale, inhale, exhale. With lojong, everything is concise and very wisely organized by Atisha and then especially by Chekawa Yéshé Dorjé who arranged it into the seven points of mind training. The whole great, powerful practice of lojong is combined in the seven points. And through tonglen the two accumulations [of merit and wisdom] are combined together.

> [As for the latter, post-meditation, there are:]
>
> **Three objects, three poisons, three roots of good-ness**.
>
> A great many beings develop attachment, aversion, and ignorance because they find objects to be attractive, unappealing, or in between. Therefore, imagine that once their three poisons have dissolved into you, they become endowed with the three roots of goodness free from attachment, aversion, and mental opacity.

So from time to time, recite these three points: three objects, three poisons, three roots of goodness. Three are the result, three are the cause, and three are the remedies.

> **Use bywords to train in every kind of activity**.
>
> Recite aloud: may all sentient beings' negativities and suffering mature in me, and may all of my happiness and goodness ripen in all sentient beings.
>
> **When taking, begin with yourself**.
>
> Through accepting right now all of the suffering that is supposed to be experienced in the future, may I also be able to relieve others of their pain

by having my karma ripen here during this life. This is

SESSION 2

one of the attitudes you should have when you do the tonglen practice. Is it clear for you?

> The **third point** is **transforming adverse circumstances into the path** towards enlightenment.
>
> **When the whole world is filled with iniquity, transform adverse circumstances into the path of awakening.**
>
> When the karmic consequences of iniquity ripen, the resources of the outer container—the world—degenerate, and its occupants—sentient beings—misbehave. Integrate this situation into the path through both attitude and deeds.
>
> To transform the first of these, [your attitude], through conventional bodhicitta:

We all experience that there are so many bad things happening in the world now. Maybe in past centuries even worse things happened; compared to that, maybe it is better now. But still, a lot of bad things are happening in the world.

There is individual karma and there is common karma. Common karma is common in the sense that we all experience this world; we are sharing the illusion of this world due to the same karma. Individually, when problems occur—like floods, earthquakes, hurricanes, tornadoes, fires, war, or hijacked airplanes—some of us are victims and some are not. The victims have to face and experience these troubles due to their individual karma. When there is less support of merit, some will experience all the troubles while others, who have more support of merit, will not experience them. Common karma and individual karma.

Nevertheless, everything is caused by what?

Student: Attachment.

Attachment, yes. The first attachment is self-clinging, the feeling or thinking in terms of "I." All sentient beings have that feeling of "I"—it is invisible. It is not that someone taught you to think "*me*." No. Every living being naturally has the concept of "I." This is the beginning, the root of samsara, individually and commonly. Every one of us has it. Then that attitude grows and then you say, "*My* form! *My* physical form!" But how? Where? If you search for something real that you can attach yourself to, something that you can reasonably grasp, you cannot find anything that your mind can reasonably cling to.

The physical form grows and gets old gradually, and eventually you will die. You don't have good reasons to cling to it so strongly, but you do because naturally you have self-clinging. When you cannot share your happiness with others, it is because of self-clinging. If we do not share with one another, it's because each of us has self-clinging.

There is an esoteric Vajrayana practice that can change your physical form into a rainbow form[2] before you die, and you attain enlightenment. This can be accomplished through Vajrayogini practice. I heard that even scientifically it's been proven that one can do it. I understand Vajrayana philosophy to be very close to neurology and other sciences.

So, two lamas received Vajrayogini instructions from

2   For this practice, Rainbow Body (Tib. *'ja' lus*), highly accomplished Vajrayana practitioners train in using their physical bodies as instruments of spiritual transformation in such a way that when they die, rainbows and lights are visible in the environment, and the corpse shrinks and sometimes disappears. In this story, the spiritual power of the "non-attached" practitioner is such that he disappears into full realization of the rainbow body while still alive.

their teacher, and then they practiced together. They were committed to staying in retreat and vowed that they would not come out until they attained enlightenment. They were sharing food. I don't know how they got the food—maybe there was a sponsor. Then one day both of them had the same vision of climbing up a staircase; there was a rainbow staircase and they were climbing up it. One of them continued up, and the other suddenly thought that his mala[3] had fallen on the step. As he was picking it up, everything disappeared, everything was gone. His friend had disappeared and he was left there. Everything was as usual—nothing had happened to him; nothing had changed. He was so disappointed! He went to his teacher and complained, "What happened? What's going on? My friend is already gone and I have been left behind."

The teacher tried to understand what the cause of the problem was. He found out that this practitioner was more attached to the food than his friend; he ate more than his friend did. The food was given to both of them equally, but he was less polite about eating it because of his attachment, and that attachment disturbed his practice. At that moment the implementation of remedies must have been weak and therefore the attachment that was in his mind produced the illusion that he dropped his mala and was picking it up. [*chuckles*] This is a true story—it really happened!

Attachment is like that. All the problems we experience are caused by it. They are not caused by somebody or something else like a country, or individual leaders, or the mafia. Yes, on the surface the hijackers and the

---

3   Buddhist prayer beads used for practice.

others are the problem—but deep down the problem is caused by attachment. If someone had hijacked his airplane, it wouldn't have bothered Milarepa!

> **Of all that is blameworthy, focus on one thing only.**
> If there is no ego, there is no cause for suffering. Once a self is clung to, many friends and enemies appear. All jealousy towards superiors, condescension towards inferiors, and rivalry towards equals have arisen from this.

So friends are from attachment. Enemies are from attachment. Jealousy of one another is from attachment. Competition is from attachment. Everything is from attachment. Toyota company, Isuzu company, Suzuki company, Range Rover company, Mercedes company: they have a *lot* of competition among themselves, but it doesn't make any difference to Milarepa. [*laughter*]

> All self-cherishing and desire for pleasure have arisen from this. Once these have been generated, they then give rise to every form of suffering. Thus, the sole origin of suffering is ego-clinging. Now then, if there is no "I," why do we reinforce this belief in a self over and over again? When ego-clinging arises, recognize it as the enemy and get rid of it.

Get rid of it how? By implementing the accurate view of the nature of ego. Ego is one kind of thought; ego has never *existed*. When you can implement this view as soon as there is a thought of ego, you will realize ego's non-existent true nature.

> **Cultivate deep gratitude towards everyone.**
> Those who have attained Buddhahood did so by cultivating lovingkindness, compassion, generosity, and

> patience towards living beings. It follows that if there
> were no sentient beings, we could not attain enlighten-
> ment; therefore, for us, there is no difference between
> the kindness of buddhas and that of sentient beings.
> Especially, consider that all those who cause harm are
> as benevolent as spiritual friends.

Those who harm us are as benevolent as spiritual friends. Some say that the Buddha's cousin, Devadatta, was a bodhisattva because he always provided causes for the Buddha to be enlightened quicker. He had made the wish to help the Buddha become enlightened, so he always harmed him. Then Buddha had to generate patience, practice compassion, everything. Devadatta provided the causes so that the Buddha could become enlightened successfully. This [explanation of Devadatta's jealousy and famously malicious behavior towards the Buddha] makes sense also.

> To repay their beneficence, even if unable to respond
> to injury by tangibly helping them, we bring about their
> benefit by means of wishes and words.

This is training. Even if you can't do it now, you can say it and your mind will be trained. Likewise, great bodhisattvas will not run at people to give them something forcefully. It's not like missionaries who force people to accept something—Christians, Buddhists: many of them do that. Great bodhisattvas will not do that. But when great bodhisattvas hear somebody say "I need your help," the happiness that arises for them cannot be compared to other forms of happiness.

Why? Because bodhisattvas have gone through their practice and have been totally trained by it. Knowing that a living being needs their help and is requesting it makes bodhisattvas so happy because they can co-operate, they can fulfill this wish! This means that the cause—bodhicitta—can develop enough power to help limitless sentient beings, just as Buddha Amitabha could manifest a Pure Land.

By knowing the cause and having the condition—a request for help from a living being—bodhisattvas' happiness is incomparably greater even than the realization of an arhat who has entirely broken through the trap of ignorance and experienced realization, an arhat who has been totally liberated from samsaric mind. Otherwise why would bodhisattvas be so happy? It's funny, silly, yeah? Such happiness can be achieved through this kind of practice, like tonglen practice.

So when anything bad happens, you blame ego, not sentient beings, and always think that sentient beings are very kind. They are providing the causes for you to become enlightened. Like the Buddha, who managed to accomplish his practice thanks to the "harmful" efforts of his cousin, Devadatta.

| In brief, according to Langri Tangpa: |

Langri Tangpa was one of the lineage holders of lojong practice and a very, very highly qualified master of the lojong lineage.

> "Among all the many profound Dharma teachings I have consulted and perused, 'all faults are mine, all qualities belong to venerable sentient beings' is the key point. Therefore, give profit and victory to others and take loss and defeat upon yourself. Other than this, there's nothing to understand." You should practice according to this maxim.

There are yogis, totally renounced practitioners, who are immersed in this practice. Like Bodhidharma, who was from India and then later was a saint in China. He was one of them: Bodhidharma, the very hairy yogi from Madras.

There's a kind of *powa* practice where you can transfer your mind into a freshly dead body and then use that dead body as you. For example, Marpa had that powa lineage and he taught it to his son. Now, Bodhidharma was a very learned master in south India. His name was Kamalashila too—not the same Kamalashila who went to India to debate with a yogachara master who came from China, but another Kamalashila who was a Buddhist master in India. He was a good-looking man—in his village in India you had one very hairy yogi and one less hairy. [*laughter*] Bodhidharma was the handsome master who did not have so much hair.

At one point, in Bodhidharma's village there was an epidemic, and he meditated to determine what the cause was. He discovered that a python had entered the well and died there. The water had become contaminated and that was the cause of so many people getting dysentery and dying. So he wanted to remove the dead python. He knew this form of powa practice, so he entered the dead python's body and made it leave the well. Meanwhile, his handsome body was left next to the well, and the other yogi knew about it. He came and stole Bodhidharma's body! [*loud laughter*] When the master came out of the python, the very hairy yogi's body was left there! [*very loud laughter*] He was so happy. "Good! This is what I want," he thought. He took it, of course. There was no other choice, but he was very happy about it: he became the hairy one.

Then he went all the way to Tibet—he met Milarepa

and they had a contest. After he spent some time in Tibet, he then went to China, to the Five Mountains. He was a great enlightened master, so the Emperor invited him to the palace and asked him to teach. Bodhidharma didn't say any words—he just shut his mouth and looked at the Emperor's face, then he stood up and walked out. He went to the mountains and meditated there. Later he taught Ch'an meditation.

So this is how you exchange and give benefit to others. Bodhidharma thought that other sentient beings were the ones who had to win the final victory, but at the same time he also won. The other yogi continued to teach—people thought he was Bodhidharma himself, so the yogi who had stolen his body carried on as a master and was quite successful. Okay? [*laughs*] This is how you implement relative bodhicitta through lojong practice!

> To transform adverse circumstances into the path through ultimate bodhicitta, as is taught:
>
> **Meditate on appearances arising from confusion as being the four kayas: emptiness is the supreme protection**.

This, of course, is very advanced practice.

> All forms of suffering and undesirable circumstances emerge from the mind's confused projections. Yet the very nature of confusion is wisdom. Observe the essence of suffering. Since it does not arise from anywhere at all, it is dharmakaya, the dimension of absolute reality.

This means that the essence of suffering is unborn. The suffering—or whatever—arises, but if you search for the source, it is not there.

> Since there is nothing that will cease, it is sambhoga-
> kaya, the dimension of perfect enjoyment.

Because mind is unobstructed, you can generate experiences on the basis of it: this is sambhogakaya, the "dimension of perfect enjoyment." It is the self-realization
that once you have achieved dharmakaya, you also have
the dimension of perfect enjoyment. It is not that you
yourself are still stuck in suffering while you are helping
others. It is not that.

> Since in between there is nothing that abides, it is nir-
> manakaya, the dimension of emanation. Since these
> kayas are indivisible, it is svabhavikakaya, the dimension
> of the essential nature.

About the three kayas: dharmakaya means the realization of the unborn nature of mind. Let's say that right
now you haven't realized the unborn nature of mind, but
still the skill and creativity of mind are there. Through
this, your mind generates all kinds of experiences of sa-
mara. You have the experience of a universe, and different kinds and forms of living beings. You share karma
with many other living beings or you do not share karma with many other living beings, and yet you are all
commonly in the realm of sentient beings through the
experience of the mind. Why? Because the mind is not
obstructed by itself, so all kinds of things and experiences can be generated and develop in the mind.

When you have fully realized the unborn nature of
mind, then all the confusion, all the so-to-say impure
manifestations, become different. To you, everything—
what you see, what you experience—has ceased to be
impure because the root has changed: from ignorance it

has become awakening. So when you can develop awakening fully, then that awakening is no longer trapped through [perceptions related to] the faculties and the consciousnesses.

Therefore, for example, Milarepa can appear in the horn of a yak and his disciple Rechungpa can see clearly that Milarepa is in the horn. . . but neither has Milarepa shrunk nor has the horn been enlarged.[4] The reason, for Milarepa, is that he is beyond limitations. At his level of equanimity, there is neither small nor big: he's out of that trap. His body manifests in the small horn of the yak, yet neither the body nor the horn is real, existing. Once this has been realized, it *is* like that. Rechungpa sees that one is big and the other is small—but the big in the small is too contradictory! For Milarepa, it is not contradictory: it is the nature of phenomena.

If everything that you see and experience is part of nirmanakaya, like Milarepa appearing in a horn, this means that help can be provided. It's like when Buddha Amitabha manifests a pure realm for sentient beings. The pure land actually arises in the minds of sentient beings, not in the mind of a buddha. Through the merit that the buddha has dedicated, his wishes are achieved. They are achieved through the capacity of his realization, his no-longer-trapped mind, his totally liberated mind. When Milarepa manifests in the horn and Buddha Amitabha manifests in a pure land, these manifesta-

---

4   In this very famous Tibetan story, the great master Milarepa teaches his disciple Rechungpa a lesson about relativity, perception, and Rechungpa's own spiritual arrogance and limitations by taking refuge inside a hollow yak horn during a hail storm. Milarepa seems to tease Rechungpa by singing, "If you think you can match your Guru, You may come into this horn. Come in right now—Here is a spacious and comfortable house! If one's mind can master the domain of space, He can enter this horn and enjoy it. Come in right now, my son, your father is calling!" (translation Garma C. C. Chang, *The Hundred Thousand Songs of Milarepa*)

tions carry the same nature, the same quality.

The nature of phenomena is not what we see now. When the unborn nature of mind is fully realized, that realization will influence all of your experiences. Each so-called illusion carries the same quality: the same pure quality of the true unborn nature of mind. Everything that we see provides the same realization, no difference.

Still human language is cat's language when explaining dharmakaya, sambhogakaya, nirmanakaya. All human language is limited like a cat's language. Meow— like that. [*laughter*] But that's how you figure it out, okay? When your mind is in the dualistic process, what do you see? When the mind is in its non-dualistic nature, what does it influence? It carries the same nature. What you see, what you experience now. Okay?

Of course, you will be able to develop this meditation only after you have experienced the unborn nature of mind. These seven points of mind training are arranged progressively. When you have accomplished realization of the unborn nature of mind, you can apply it to every phenomenon: all phenomena can be experienced as the four kayas. That means that everything can be useful. It may not be so clear to us now, but you can receive these instructions as a lineage transmission and then, like seeds growing, they will sprout and mature.

After they have been successful in the meditation, many meditators say, "Why didn't I understand when you were explaining it to me? I wonder why I did not understand at that time." You will. You *will* understand how all phenomena function as the four kayas.

When the Sakyapa give instructions for the tantras, first they want the students to understand that everything they see is nirmanakaya. When they can understand that, then naturally they will understand sambhogakaya and dharmakaya. First is nirmanakaya. As Milarepa told Gampopa, "I've already introduced you to seeing that all phenomena are like nirmanakaya. You will realize sambhogakaya and dharmakaya by yourself; there's no need to rely on my instructions."

My great wish is that all the practitioners here who receive the lineage transmission will absorb it and have this experience sooner or later. That is my wish. It will happen.

> Second, transforming adverse circumstances into the path through accumulation and purification practices:
>
> **The supreme method is comprised of the four activities.**
>
> The first of these is the activity of accumulating merit. Whenever you feel that you would like to be happy, consider that this wish for happiness is a sign that you should accumulate merit, the cause of happiness. Accumulate merit through body, speech, and mind by making offerings to the lama —

this means from whom you received the precious lineage transmission

> — and the three jewels, serving the sangha, offering *tormas* to elemental spirits, and so on.

Elemental spirits are the many semi-ghost kinds of living beings who can potentially help you. They can be helpful to your practice, like the five sisters who were very helpful to Milarepa. The five sisters were deities.

One semi-ghost helped Buddha's cousin Ananda. Do you know that story? After Buddha passed away, his disciple Kashyapa took the responsibility of organizing the first council in Rajgir in order to compile and organize the Buddha's teachings. For certain auspicious reasons, the presence of five hundred arhats was required, but one was missing. Kashyapa understood that Ananda, Buddha's younger cousin, was ready to become enlightened but he needed a cause. What was the cause? Ananda had to be badly disappointed.[5] Then he would meditate and become enlightened very quickly.

So Kashyapa put ten points of blame on him, saying that one day Ananda did not offer water to the Buddha, and he did not serve the Buddha properly, and this and that up to ten accusations, and he kicked Ananda out of the sangha community! Ananda had to walk away—he was so sad—and go to an isolated area. Then a kind of semi-ghost appeared and said, "Why are you so sad? You should meditate now. Why linger on your sadness like that? That's not the right way! You are a disciple of the Buddha, so why don't you meditate?" The semi-ghost encouraged Ananda so that he meditated and became liberated quickly: Ananda became an arhat. Then he understood that Kashyapa had just made it all up for the sake of his practice.

After that they organized the first council, and Ananda was the one who recited the sutras; Kashyapa himself was the one who recited the abhidharma. Upali revived the vinaya.

There are many of these kinds of spirits who can help your Dharma practice, so you should dedicate tormas to them: offering tormas. Do you know tormas? Cake— cheesecake. [*laughter*]

---

5   Different stories relate how it happened that Ananda was able to attain enlightenment just before the First Council convened. The visit of a "spirit" or "deity" who gave him advice while he was meditating in solitude is a common feature.

> Having fervently prayed to the lama and the three jewels, say: "If it is preferable that I be sick, pray grant the blessing of illness; if it is preferable that I recover, pray grant the blessing of healing; if it is preferable that I die, pray grant the blessing of death."
>
> The second is the activity of purifying negativities. Whenever you feel that you would like to be free from suffering, consider that this is a sign that you should abandon the cause of suffering: misdeeds. Confess those of the past with remorse, resolve to not commit others in the future, and strive to forsake negative actions through the many available methods.

The many available methods include Dorjé Sempa practice, or Thirty-Five Buddhas practice, or building a stupa. There are many, many ways to purify negativities. Also, giving food or protection to animals. Whoever is suffering most, you should help them: this is the most effective of methods.

> The third is making offerings to malevolent forces. Whenever obstacles arise due to malevolent and obstructing forces, offer them [the ritual dough objects called] tormas with a deeply grateful frame of mind. Otherwise, if this much is impossible, as you offer tormas say: "Do not create obstacles to my Dharma practice. I will do whatever I can to help you."

Ghosts are always suffering, so when you treat them nicely they are very happy and will be helpful. When people don't know how to treat ghosts properly, the ghosts become crazy. For example, some weaker-minded people who lack merit can become possessed by ghosts and then they shoot people. These things happen: evil ghosts. If you generate compassion and they receive the blessing of your compassion, then they are happy.

If you look at what is happening often in the U.S.A., I always think that one bad ghost is moving everywhere in the United States and possessing weak people who then shoot students and terrible things like that. I've been trying to offer him tormas, but I haven't found him yet. I have to make a lot of prayers for that. I wish that it will stop.

Anyway, good ghosts, bad ghosts or whatever, compassion is the way to help them. Treat them nicely instead of being angry with them. If you keep making good wishes for the ghosts and really seriously generate compassion, then they get help and will be very helpful for practitioners too. Tibetan people really believe in ghosts; they are bothered a lot by them. That's why these Kadam masters pay attention to the people's belief in ghosts. They also live in very isolated areas and ghosts are usually wandering in those isolated areas. [*laughs*] Tibet has more ghosts than London! [*laughter*] Ghosts are very shy and they cannot go into a house where there is a lot of furniture. They always go into houses which have no furniture; lonely houses are their homes. So when you see any haunted house, use it for generosity and make good wishes for the ghosts. Make the haunter your friend for your Dharma practice!

The fourth is making offerings to the Dharma protectors. As you offer them tormas, pray that all circumstances which hinder Dharma practice are pacified and favorable conditions are established.

Join unexpected events with your practice.

If unexpected tribulations such as illness, negative forces, enemies, and so forth befall you all of a sudden,

> think with the utmost sincerity: "In our universe, there is
> no end to the different kinds of intense suffering similar
> to this. May they all gather into myself."

This is a great way to dedicate yourself for others. Once you can really, sincerely make a wish like this, then sentient beings will truly be helped, I think. Even lions and leopards in safari jungles have compassion nowadays. You often see this on the animal channels—when they see baby animals, they protect them. You can really directly see it. I have offered tormas to save a baby deer from the river. The baby deer was looking for its mother when a lion came; at first the lion wanted to attack the fawn. Then it realized that the deer was a baby; it protected it and gave it food.

This is happening nowadays. I think that all this is happening because many, many people in the world are concerned about animal suffering, and there's the merit of compassion. A great deal of compassion is generated by people, which is very good. Compassion carries a lot of blessings, so naturally many living beings absorb these blessings and their minds develop compassion too. I believe that.

Thank you, I will stop here today and continue tomorrow.

Session 3

The **fourth point** shows how to **incorporate the practice in one's lifetime.**

The epitome of the pith instructions is the application of the five powers.

The first is the compelling power. Compel your mind forcefully thus: "From now on—this month, this year, until I die, until I have reached Buddhahood—I will never be separated from the two aspects of awakening mind."

The second is the power of familiarization. Train again and again in both [ultimate and relative] bodhicittas.

The third is the power of sowing white seeds. Accumulate merit by doing everything you can to generate and enhance awakening mind.

The term "power" means that your mind has to have a strong habit of spontaneously implementing these positive qualities at the time when they are required. You need willpower to follow these commitments. Cheka-wa Yéshé Dorjé himself accomplished everything within thirteen years—he attained enlightenment. This is a very short time to achieve such realization; it very much depends upon implementing these powers. If you do implement them, your practice can be very successful. Without them, you will linger on for a longer time. If you are lacking these powers, then such realization within a lifetime will be difficult.

Of course, in some lifetimes, you can achieve realization because of the power of merit. Seven-point mind training is a very, very condensed collection of powerful bodhisattva practices. The mind training practice is directed towards attaining at least the first bhumi within one life, but if you don't apply these powers constantly, you may not be able to achieve this. I think the first, second, and third powers are presented here quite simply. Is it clear? Yes, it is clear to you.

| The fourth is the power of disenchantment. |

The moment a snake comes into your lap, you will remove it and the snake will not have time to bite you. The moment your hair catches fire, you should put it out so the fire will not grow. If you are too late, if you wait too long, things will be more difficult. At the very moment, at the very beginning when a cherishing-your-self thought appears, you have to step on it, put it out!

You have to implement a remedy immediately. Many learned practitioners are not successful because they do not take measures in the beginning when a problem appears, like Mahadeva, a Buddhist monk who started a different sect. The main reason was that he and a friend of his disagreed on some points and their teacher, a Buddhist master, said that the friend was right. Mahadeva was so angry that he stabbed the teacher and was banished from the community. He had to flee and went to a different place.

Mahadeva had so many regrets about his bad karmic actions. He built a temple, collected disciples, and taught them Buddhism. He was learned and he taught very well, but he had a very strong attachment to himself, to his fame, and so on. In the nighttime when he was alone, he would think about all of his past mistakes and he couldn't control his regrets. He would weep and shout that he had done a very bad thing. In the morning, when his disciples would gather and ask him why he had been crying so loudly last night, he wasn't able to say that he was remembering his mistakes and regretting his karma. He couldn't admit that. Instead, he said, "I was thinking about the suffering of sentient beings and therefore I cried."

Cherishing yourself is a very big disturbance. You have to subdue it from the beginning. Use the methods to subdue it in this way:

> When self-cherishing arises, respond with the thought: "In the past, I have met with suffering because of this, and in this life too it precludes the [practice of] Dharma," and do away with it.
>
> The fifth is the power of aspirations. Following all virtuous practices, recite this aspiration prayer: "May I never be separated from awakening mind, and may I apply myself wholeheartedly to enlightened activities. Now that the buddhas have taken me in their care, may the maras' actions be dispelled." Pray to the lama and the three jewels that this will happen as expressed.

These are all Shantideva's prayers. As I already explained, the images that exist in the consciousnesses of sentient beings do not exist independently by themselves outside of their minds—everything is happening *within* the beings' minds. By knowing the causes, the reasons for the appearance of sentient beings' illusions, you will be able to engage with them and transform them into positive illusions. The right causes—meritorious actions in what you say, what you do, and what you think—must be fully influenced by bodhicitta mind. When everything you say or do is done with the attitude of bodhicitta, nothing can go wrong; merit will be accumulated spontaneously.

Then the merit should be dedicated for sentient beings. In what way? Just as Buddha Amitabha dedicated all his merit for sentient beings to have a pure realm, so the bodhisattva Shantideva made a lot of wishes such as, "May I be the one who helps sentient beings who are suffering in realms like hell." Not only that, but he was also thinking of even the small, small problems of sentient beings and making wishes that he would be the one who could solve them.

Like for sailors, when they have lost their direction, "I should be there as an island where they can land. If travelers need a bridge, I should appear as a bridge so they can cross the river. If a patient is suffering without helpers, I should be a nurse for them." During the Second World War there were volunteer nurses who helped so many victims. I heard about a British noblewoman who contributed her energy to be a nurse for those patients. It's that kind of wish.

"Now that the buddhas have taken me into their care" doesn't mean that a buddha is a kind of god who thinks, "Oh, now she is calling me, so I should provide help." According to this precise view, of course, you can have a god like that, but not necessarily. Here, it doesn't mean that you're calling to the buddhas to care for you. No, it is not like that. Because of the power of your merit, you are able to absorb the blessings of the buddhas and the wishes that buddhas had dedicated for sentient beings when they were bodhisattvas. Therefore, "may the maras'[6] actions be dispelled. Pray to the lama and the three jewels that this will happen as expressed."

> **The Mahayana instructions for dying are the same five powers. Conduct is essential.**
> For the power of sowing white seeds, give away everything you own as offerings and donations.

Many lamas, many good practitioners, give away everything before they die. . . and then they get well again. [*laughter*] This has happened quite a number of times. [*laughter continues*] In any case, when it's pretty sure that you will die, then give everything away. There's nothing to be attached to. Be free of attachment.

> For the power of aspirations, pray to the lama and three jewels and formulate the wish to perfectly accomplish bodhicitta.

Pray to the lama from whom you received the bodhisattva vows as well as the practice instructions. The three jewels are the Buddha, Dharma, and Sangha.

---

6   Mara is the embodiment of the forces—internal and external—that keep beings stuck in samsara, the state of suffering. Translated as "demon," "trickster," "tempter/temptress," etc., Mara could be seen as the guardian of the afflictions and of the cycle of birth and death. Mara famously fails in his attempt to persuade, then force, the Buddha to abandon his quest for enlightenment.

> For the power of disenchantment, think: "Even now I have been suffering because of clinging to the idea of a cherished self in this body. But when examined, there is nothing whatsoever which is a 'self.'" With this, self-clinging will surely cease.

Using logic to think that there is no self to cling to is one way to do this. But another way is using the *feeling* of the self as the subject that you should examine. All living beings naturally have a feeling of "I myself." You should focus your meditation on that *feeling* of self. Is that clear to you?

Logically, yes, you can ask "where is self?" Many Hindu sects say that self is there as an aura, that a greater self exists. The artificial self is not really there, they say, but a "great self" is there, and without this "great self" one is lost. There's a kind of forceful logic that these Hindu sects use when they debate with others; they have opinions about how to defend their view of a self. But if you do your own searching based on the *feeling* of self, you don't have to rely on someone else's logic: you yourself can discover whether there is a self or no self.

Without a *feeling* of a self, why would sentient beings assume that there *is* a self? It's because of that feeling that you assume that there is "your" self. If you search, if you examine the feeling of a self, that feeling does not exist independently. It is one thought, one concept, one of many feelings.

So here, at the moment when you are dying, you can be sure to cut through self-clinging thanks to your habit of being aware of selflessness.

> For the compelling power, think: "I will train in awakening mind during the bardo and the next lives."

Already now, you should be clear about always remembering that bodhicitta practice is required at all times, including during the bardo. By assembling many positive causes, such as gathering merit and emphasizing the importance of bodhicitta in your mind, then when your mind starts wandering in the bardo, you will recognize that that's where you are—in the bardo—and you will continue to practice bodhicitta there. So you train in that motivation and determination first, now, before it's time to do the lojong tradition powa at the moment of death.

> As for the power of familiarization, begin with purification via the relative bodhicitta practice of tonglen that rides the breath.

Regarding tonglen, in most lojong traditions it is best-known as a relative bodhicitta practice. But in some lojong traditions, it is mentioned that you should combine it with absolute bodhicitta. I think generally tonglen is considered relative bodhicitta because those who have no realization of mind-nature can do tonglen practice. But if you can maintain the realization of mind-nature when you are working or talking with somebody, then why not combine that realization with tonglen practice?

For good meditators who already know how to sit in the realization of mind-nature, combining that realization and tonglen is very simple. Then tonglen practice no longer remains as relative bodhicitta. Of course, beginners should not try to force the mind into that realization while they are driving, for example. But when there's no danger, they can try to implement it.

I've told you that the combined practice is the cause for developing sambhogakaya and nirmanakaya. When your dharmakaya meditation integrates sambhogakaya and nirmanakaya, you will not be stuck in dharmakaya realization alone. Certain Dharma schools, like Hinayana, don't go into bodhicitta practice. They are stuck in dharmakaya realization and do not try to keep going after liberation is attained. They look to cut though the root of samsara: self-clinging. Of course, they develop enormous power from that: having cut through self-clinging, they become free from samsara. But they will be stuck in that realization.

Bodhisattvayana practitioners adopt bodhisattva practices. They go through the combined accumulation practices in order to achieve full Buddhahood. This means that their realization of dharmakaya is complete, and in addition they will be able to visibly manifest their wishes for sentient beings in sambhogakaya and nirmanakaya.

So here, when you do the tonglen that rides the breath, your tonglen should be influenced by the realization of mind-nature.

> Then, settle within the meditative equipoise of ultimate bodhicitta free from any conceptual grasping.

When you have realized the nature of mind, you see that *all* concepts are connected to something that you are grasping. With this awareness, thoughts will not be trapped in these concepts.

> Conduct entails lying on the right side of the body with your right hand supporting your cheek. Block the right nostril with your little finger so that your breath comes and goes from your left nostril.

When I die I will use *this* finger because I don't have long fingers. [*laughter*]

Make the wish that you will recognize your bardo state and that you will practice bodhicitta in the bardo state. That is your goal, one hundred percent. There's nothing that you will need to be concerned about because of the certainty that your mind is free from every attachment to your belongings and everything else. You have no use for them.

Because you can use every concept that arises to realize its nature, you will be free from disturbances. Then, with this conduct, you can simply let your mind stop existing in its present form. Let it be, just like that. Of course, you can make any other wishes simultaneously in whatever way you want, such as, "I will come back to this world again to save sentient beings." You can make wishes according to the needs of sentient beings.

What do you think is the biggest problem of sentient beings in this world now? Remember the five degenerations? In the 17th century, there was a very, very famous yogi named Kathog Rigzin Chenpo who was deeply involved in the Nyingma and Kagyu lineages. He was very learned, especially in the subject of Kalachakra. Already at that time, he claimed that the lifespan degeneration was taking place. He said that soon, people would live for only about thirty or forty years. I think that nowadays it is not that—nowadays it is getting better; we're not falling into the degeneration of lifespan. Life expectancy is growing and improving.

When I was young, the faces of forty-year-olds were full of wrinkles, but nowadays not. [*laughter*] So lifespan is increasing. But still, you could say that we have many, many degenerations; many, many problems in this life. So if any bodhisattvas die [and make wishes to come back and benefit beings], what wishes should they make to solve the problems of the world now—to stop war? There's less of a danger of war than in former times, isn't there? I think so. Nowadays no one wants a big war like the First World War or the Second World War. . . except for a few countries in the world. [*laughter*]

The degeneration of religion may be one of the biggest problems that we are facing now. In former times, there was superstition in some European countries—a lot of women were accused as witches and burned alive. Even in Buddhist countries like Tibet, they always looked down on women—they didn't burn women, but they made them lower. In Nepal and India it was terrible: *sati*—burning widows through the influence of religion—was a tradition there. In Nepal, sati was conducted officially, but in India I think that it was the husband and family circle that encouraged the woman to die in the flames of her husband's funeral cremation. These are examples of the degeneration of some religions. This degeneration is really growing in the world nowadays. Maybe not in the same way, but women are still being stoned to death, and it is happening in the name of religion.

The degeneration of view or degeneration of discrimination is less prevalent now, isn't it? Tibetan lamas are not discriminated against I don't think. Before, different races, like black people, were looked down upon, badly. But nowadays we don't have that, do we? We gave that up; we respect everyone equally. No one in the west discriminates between black and white now, do they? [*audience: maybe not officially. . .*] But unofficially, I see. [*laughter*] Lama Tenzin Wangpo, do you discriminate about colors? No? Congratulations. [*laughter*] Anyway, think about the root of sentient beings' troubles and find a way to solve the problem, okay? And whoever can do so should make wishes.

As for reincarnation, one has to reincarnate to accomplish one's wish. Recognizing reincarnates is not about protecting the wealth of a certain kind of lama. No, sorry! It's about making wishes for sentient beings. Then, like here in the text, there's the Mahayana powa which means you will reincarnate. Before you die, if you go through this practice, you will definitely reincarnate according to your wish.

> As for propitious substances, thoroughly grind a powder of magnetite —

Magnetite is a metal and you grind it. Not very necessary, but you can use it

> — and burnt cowry shells, mix it with wild honey, and make pea-size pills beforehand.

According to the biology of the Medicine Buddha, mind is actually clinging to all the nervous systems in the body. The nervous systems in the body have many levels; among them all, the subtlest part is the most strongly grasped. The mind rides the energy [of the nervous system] and goes everywhere simultaneously.

I've participated in neuroscientific investigations into mind; how mind works with the body. Of course, I had already learned about how Buddhists think. But lately I have also read a lot about what neuroscientists think and we have exchanged views. I believe that this is partially understood by neuroscience.

According to Vajrayana, the energy that is flowing, circulating through the nervous system carries mind.

Mind is combined with it. It is very important to open up this part [*indicates the fontanelle at the top of the head*]—when you are dying, your mind will leave from here.

This understanding has been developed in an extreme way; some religious masters have misused it in order to discriminate among the races or castes. For example, Hindus say that Brahma is the creator god, and Brahmins, the highest caste, emerged from Brahma's head. This subject has different interpretations. Some non-Brahmins—I think that all of us here are non-Brahmins [*laughter*]—dropped from the shaking feet of Brahma, who saw that Brahmins needed servants, workers, and laborers. The high caste is supreme and its members are worshiped. Of course, this has been used politically. These kinds of things happen in the world.

The reality is that up here is the right channel that mind should exit from. One channel is here at the forehead, and when it is opened then there is a third eye. Lobsang Rangpa wrote this as fiction but actually this view exists in Vajrayana. If you know anatomy, then you know it is there—one channel is there. Here, you don't have to open your third eye, but you do open the top channel here, at the fontanelle, and then you make wishes. The substances [mentioned above] can help with that.

The 13th Karmapa, Düdül Dorjé, wrote in his autobiography about a time when he did powa for a man but it was very difficult for the practice to have the proper effect. Then he understood that the man had had too much tobacco—Tibetans are always sniffing snuff—and that it had damaged the man's nervous system. Tobacco is not good for the health, but it can be an imperfect replacement for drugs like cocaine and hashish—a compromise. [*laughter*] However, it does block the nervous system, so it is not so good. The 13th Karmapa Düdül Dorjé couldn't do powa very well for that man because he had had too much tobacco and it was blocking circulation in the subtle *nadis*.[7] Because the circulation was broken, the practice couldn't go through properly.

Vajrayana philosophy and medical science agree that mind has some very subtle substance. Mahayana says empty, empty, empty, but in Vajrayana, it's like there is a little bit of substance. Of course, it carries the nature of being free from the dualistic process of confused mind, but in Vajrayana theory and medical science, mind isn't completely empty like space. Medicine Buddha teachings explain that mind travels with the energy in the subtle channels, the nadis. Good scholars can explain clearly and without contradictions the Mahayana view of mind and the medical subject of Medicine Buddha. I'm not good on that, but I do know that there are differences, and that they do not contradict each other.

> When the moment of death is nigh, mix them with ale and rub some on the crown of the head.

The 5th Shamarpa does not know vodka, so he uses the word *chang*. [*laughter*] Any chang is okay—in Tibetan *chang* means alcohol. I think the alcohol should be from barley or millet or other grains, not synthetic alcohol.

The "crown of the head" means four fingers back from the edge of the forehead, [the fontanelle]. But it is not really necessary; if you are good at the practice

---

7   The nadis are the channels of the subtle energy body within the physical body. A living being's subtle body is where the immaterial mind and the material body interact.

of lojong, that is the most important thing. If you have the substances it's fine, but I don't think it is advisable to have a factory for that [*laughter*].

> The **fifth point** presents how to **evaluate progress in mind training**.
> **All Dharma is united in one objective**.
> In Mahayana and Hinayana traditions alike, the objective of all forms of the Dharma involves subduing ego-clinging. If Dharma has not been effective as an antidote to ego, then our entire practice has been useless. If it has been effective as an antidote, then lojong—mind training—has truly dawned within us.

Here, when we say Mahayana, Vajrayana is included. In the West and in non-Tibetan, non-Himalayan areas, Vajrayana may be considered something separate from Mahayana. But sometimes when we say Mahayana, Vajrayana is included. Hinayana is, yes, somewhat different since, as I explained, it's the vehicle that is entirely focused on cutting through the self.

In Buddhist practice, liberation results from the elimination of self-clinging. Self-clinging manifests in many different ways; you yourself should know whether you really have contained your self-clinging or not.

> **Of two witnesses, heed the more important one**.
> If your general appearance is such that others see you as a practitioner and respect you, it is indeed a testimony, but not the most important one. Ordinary people cannot read your thoughts; if they happen to catch you engaging in positive conduct, they may be quite impressed. But you know if you have nothing to be ashamed of; therefore, the most important witness is you.

In the Himalayas, when Buddhist communities analyze whether someone is the right teacher, the right practitioner, or not, they generally look very closely at how they live. They don't simply follow what they say. They look at their behavior, everyday conduct, and character; they analyze whether the person has really renounced or not. They analyze a lot. But that is not so important, is it?

Whether others respect you and consider you to be a genuine practitioner may be important for them, but for you, it is not important. *You* know if you have nothing to be ashamed of. *You* should be the witness as to whether you have really contained and subdued the ego or not. *You* should know if there is nothing to regret, nothing to change. Therefore the most important witness is yourself. As Chekawa said, "Were I to die this instant, I would have no regrets." This means, "From the great intention that I practice, I follow the methods of selflessness and now I won't regret if I die at this moment. I am my own witness."

Many genuine practitioners keep a low profile, and then they test themselves to see how they react in difficult situations in order to see if they have subdued ego or not. For example, they'll go into a crowd to test whether they mind if somebody spits on them or anything like that.

There was a highly respected Drukpa Kagyu lama in Sikkim whom I remember very well. Lopön-la was always practicing meditation in the north of Sikkim. He kept a very low profile, but people knew that he was a really great lama. One year, he came to see the 16th Karmapa at the time of the summer dances. He was in the front of the crowd when some people behind him stood up and ran towards the Karmapa to get his blessing. They pushed him to the front and he stumbled and hit the Karmapa's table and some objects; some designs there were broken. One of the secretaries slapped him—I was there. This lama did not mind at all—he thanked him! Then later the secretary realized that he was a very respected lama and went to ask for his forgiveness. Lopön-la said to him, "You purified my bad karma. I'm not angry at all. I am so sorry; I did not do it intentionally. But Karmapa's throne is so great—I misbehaved by being pushy." Deeply he was not irritated or upset even though he was highly respected by many, many Kagyu lamas.

This general secretary of the Karmapa was not usually very religious. He was devoted only to Karmapa and not to the other lamas. Everybody else knew that the lama was a well-known practitioner of lojong and mahamudra combined—but the secretary didn't and he slapped him, which was quite rude. And Lopön-la *really* did not mind.

> **An ever-serene mind is the only recourse.**
> From now on, even if a calamitous situation were to arise, it would be acceptable because you could incorporate it into the path of mind training. With this thought, nothing poses a threat, so relax.

Chöd practitioners have to go into sky burial sites and do chöd in the nighttime. Western cemeteries are very well-decorated, so I would not be afraid there. [*laughter*] But in Tibet, sky burial sites have bloody stones everywhere and you have to go at night to do the practice. Tibetan parents always tell ghost stories to their children—ghosts, ghosts, ghosts—and in Tibet, the isolated areas and charnel grounds where they do chöd practice are very scary. But the practitioners recall their lojong practice. They think, "I have already dedicated my body as a feast for the ghosts, so what do I have to fear?" When they remember that, they relax.

Chöd is an esoteric practice where you visualize yourself as a big feast for the ghosts, then you invite them to come participate in the feast. In Tibet, chöd practitioners blow human thigh bones because if you blow a human thigh bone, ghosts will come—ghosts have a habit of responding to the call of the human thigh bone. Indian yogis come to Kailash and die there, then Tibetan nomads remove their thigh bones to use in chöd practice because yogis have some blessings, plus they have very straight thigh bones which blow very well! [*laughter*] Chöd was not usually an official monastic ritual because it is an "undignified" practice where they blow into a thigh bone and play a very large damaroo or hand-drum. It was mostly practiced in hermitages.

Ghosts—most people believe in ghosts, right? I think so, because many people see ghosts. Especially, old cities like London or Manchester will have many ghosts because many, many buildings are haunted. In your history you have had many wars and people died badly.

In this practice you are surrounded by ghosts and then you do tonglen, giving all of your happiness and causes of happiness to others, as always, and relieving them of their suffering by absorbing it all into yourself. Once you are involved in this practice, this dedication of happiness, what is there to be afraid of? Usually fear is about you yourself. It comes from a need to protect yourself from danger, but now, due to selflessness, you have nothing to protect. Your chöd will be very successful if you can implement selflessness in this way.

Lojong practice is the same: if you are totally free

from self-clinging, happiness will prevail. Usually, all worries arise from self-clinging. But you have nothing to protect yourself from: you are free! You are in a state of mind which is totally free from self-clinging. There is great joy because you are released from the trap in which you had been caught since beginningless lifetimes up until now. Now you are out of it, so of course there's a lot of freedom and joy there: a joy that can't be described in human words. It's like when I said that our human language is like a cat's language for explaining the experience of wisdom. Here too you are experiencing wisdom, therefore you will consistently have happiness in the mind.

> **If you are able even when distracted, you have trained well**.
>
> Even when distracted, able riders do not fall from their horses. Similarly, even when harm-doers and their like suddenly appear, if we do not experience anger but use [the situation] to enhance our lojong practice, the mind has been well-trained.

Junior practitioners may have to concentrate very hard to think about selflessness if they accidentally meet someone who wants to do or does them harm. Intermediate practitioners may be shocked for a while, but then they will be able to think over what happened. They will remember their lojong practice and then they won't be angry; they will not mind any more. For those who are well-trained, completely trained, everything can be integrated into the practice. If anyone harms them, instead of becoming angry or intolerant, they will go into the practice instantaneously. The situation will help them increase the strength of their practice. Of course, as lojong always says, you should be your own best witness so you will know [how well you are integrating the situation into your practice].

> These evaluations of training show whether lojong has developed in your mind, but that does not mean that when one has "trained well," one need train no longer. Training must continue until Buddhahood has been achieved!

Yes, training will continue but there's no need to force things; without forcing, training opportunities will come. Many bodhisattvas welcome unnecessary enemies in order to expand their practice of patience. Like the Buddha—even as a young man, before he was enlightened, he was never angry about his cousin's attacks. His cousin always tried to do all kinds of things to harm him and attack him, but the Buddha was never angry or enraged. The Buddha was a prince at that time and he had no teacher to guide his practice, but of course he had been a bodhisattva for many eons. So he was already a qualified bodhisattva and could apply the remedy spontaneously.

> The **sixth point** presents the lojong precepts.
>
> ### Always train in the three basic principles.
>
> The first basic principle concerns not transgressing your commitments. If you call yourself a lojong practitioner, you must not brush aside even minor precepts. From individual liberation vows to those of Vajrayana, however many precepts you have committed yourself to should be maintained faultlessly.

Some practitioners who know just a little bit think that

they are actually highly qualified and they minimize the importance of the precepts. Mahayana practitioners may think, "Yeah, I took the vows of *genyen*, *getsül*, *gelong*, whatever, but now I'm a bodhisattva so I don't have to concern myself with these precepts. They are mainly suitable for Hinayana practitioners."

Tantric practitioners might think, "I have special knowledge of how to convert all poisons into medicine, so why not?" Then they go wildly into intoxication, for example. It happens quite often that Vajrayana practitioners face obstacles like this; they are misguided by their own mistaken concepts. They don't realize their mistakes, and engage in them thinking, "I'm a great such and such. . ." However, if you have committed yourself to any precepts, they should be maintained.

Many yogis drink alcohol in order to control their minds. The point of the precept about intoxicants is that you abstain from alcohol because it will contaminate the mind; it will spoil the capacity of the mind for meditation. After you have developed very good control of meditation, then you might drink alcohol and test whether you can control the alcohol or whether alcohol is still controlling you. At that time, you should be very careful not to think, "I'm okay" [if, in fact, you are not]. That kind of thing.

"Maintaining faultlessly" means that if you took vows to not engage in stealing, but you see somebody who is in the terrible suffering of starvation and you have nothing to give them, you can go into a bakery shop—you can break in and steal some food to give them. That's okay. That is absolutely okay. But that is not a valid excuse for someone who is just being crafty: "I'm a bodhisattva, so it's okay for me to steal!" [*laughter*]

> The second basic principle concerns refraining from nonsensical behavior.

Charlatans, isn't it? Some charlatans collect wealth from people by behaving as a holy person.

> All reckless acts—such as cutting down haunted trees or keeping company with lepers in order to convince others that you are free of self-cherishing—should be abandoned.

Certain trees are believed to have been appropriated by a kind of non-human being that has made the tree their home. I told you earlier about the Buddha's cousin Ananda who was advised by a kind of semi-god or semi-ghost who lived in the woods. He appeared and asked Ananda, "Why don't you go into practice now?" There are many ghosts like that.

In Tibet, sometimes people will say, "Oh, that tree is haunted," and keep away from it. Like banyan trees—in tribal lands, banyan trees are believed to be haunted. If you cut such a tree, people think, "Wow, their power is greater than the power of the non-humans." The meaning is that ghosts must be frightened of you since you dare do such things.

Or to demonstrate their power, their high level, certain meditators might break some kind of haunted relic, like a stupa which is haunted. Then people say, "Oh, great lama, you have power!" You should not show off like that.

It's similar if someone believes, "I am free from every concept so I cannot get diseases from those who are contagious." It is not really just acting—they actually have this belief. Then, if they go into a leper colony, for example, they might catch the disease. Poor meditator! By thinking that they are great practitioners who are beyond these problems and will not get sick, they go there, get leprosy, and die.

The slogan means that you should not be wild. It is just a way of saying to the Tibetans that even though some lamas may be doing that, they should not. Do you understand?

> The third basic principle concerns not falling into partial behavior. Train in equanimity by rejecting all forms of partiality, such as being patient when people aggress you but not when gods or demons do; respecting those who are important and scorning those who are not; being kind to loved ones and hostile to enemies, and so on.

This is comprehensible, easy to understand.

> **Transform your approach while remaining natural.**
> You used to treasure yourself above all. Now that others have become more important, your physical behavior should be consistent with Dharma while remaining natural. It is said that lojong practice must be very effective yet very discreet; it should ripen in your mindstream without being obvious to others.

In order to be successful you should behave like this. Also, formerly, you yourself were the most important thing, but not anymore because you are following this powerful training.

Discreet is very good, very important—then you will not be distracted by people's respect. If people think, "Oh, you are a holy teacher," you might engage in wrong behavior because you are earning a lot of respect from them. Therefore, most of the great masters of the Kad-

am lineage—the lineage of Atisha—have kept a low profile. All the Kadam lineage teachers are very, very low
profile. They don't show off. They remain very gentle.

> **Do not speak of others' infirmities**.
> Do not use harsh words to speak of others' physical im-
> pairments, such as blindness, or Dharma-related fail-
> ings, such as unseemly moral conduct.

England is especially very good for that, isn't it? Queen
Victoria's ethical advice is good for these things, yah? In
the Buddha's time they were very good at that too. But
in one history text it does say that the established name
of one of the masters who revived all the teachings of
the Buddha was "Big Belly." I found it in a list of arhats:
Big Belly Arhat. They gave him that name! Maybe he ac-
cepted it—or maybe not.

> **Never judge others**.
> If you see others' faults, those of living beings in gen-
> eral and more specifically those of people who have
> entered the gates of the Dharma, think: "This must be
> my own impure perception—they cannot possibly have
> such faults."

The lama who received the slap from the Karmapa's secretary—I know him very well—he's very much in this,
very much. His mind is really completely trained; it has
become his real nature. It is not that he is trying. It is
completely in his nature.

> **Purify whichever affliction is the strongest first**.

In the lojong text that I arranged, I put this slogan in an

earlier section at the part where absolute bodhicitta is practiced. Many lojong texts do keep this as one of the disciplines or precepts. So, of course, it is not contradictory, but according to the practice itself, *purify whichever affliction is the strongest first* is very, very connected with absolute bodhicitta meditation.

In Hinayana, the metaphor used is like sparks flying from welding irons. When they fly, some sparks vanish up into space; for others it takes a little longer, and they only vanish when they nearly touch the ground. When you can implement absolute bodhicitta—the realization of mind's nature—on each of the afflictions and that practice becomes natural, then when any of the afflictions appear, their nature will be seen to be mind's nature. The afflictions themselves contribute to a clear understanding of their own nature. When this happens, the afflictions are not afflictions; they're realization.

Before you go into the combined practices of relative and absolute bodhicitta through tonglen practice, I think it is very important to implement absolute bodhicitta on the afflictions, so I put it at the beginning of my own commentary in the second point, because absolute bodhicitta is presented in the second point. The order of the lojong root text is not arranged strictly. You can find many different root texts, the words of one are up here, the words of another are down there. There are, I think, three or four different root texts. In the lojong root text found in the *Treasury of Oral Instructions*, for instance, there is one extra *shloka*—verse—which is not found in many other root texts.

When I wrote my lojong commentary, I rearranged it according to the sutra. Sutras are the teachings of the Buddha. According to the sutra lojong, the first preliminary practice is shiné, the second is absolute bodhicitta practice, and the third is absolute bodhicitta practice combined with relative bodhicitta. That's how you will accomplish the accumulation of the two practices in three countless *kalpas*, three countless eons.

Bodhisattvas engage in the two accumulations combined: one is the wisdom side, and the other is the relative bodhicitta practice where, for example, you are physically helping others. These are combined together *after* you have become successful in absolute bodhicitta, otherwise you will not accurately understand that everything is like a mirage. You will force yourself to think that everything is illusion-like and not real, but it won't be an authentic understanding. With some realization of absolute bodhicitta, you will *directly* experience all phenomena as being like a mirage. To be able to accumulate the two bodhicitta practices, you have to already have that realization. In order to truly put lojong into practice, having absolute bodhicitta practice go ahead of relative bodhicitta practice is very important.

[In the lojong commentary I wrote, *The Path to Awakening*,] absolute bodhicitta practice is explained in the beginning of the second point. In my book, purifying the strongest affliction first fits very naturally with absolute bodhicitta practice. Why are you doing this absolute bodhicitta practice? You need to realize the nature of mind.

The nature of mind cannot be separated from ignorance. Afflictions arise from ignorance, therefore they cannot be apart from the nature of mind. Afflictions are a kind of mind; the realization of the nature of mind and the realization of the nature of afflictions is the same. Being able to apply the absolute bodhicitta view to the afflictions is most important for practice.

> Once you have identified which of your emotional af-
> flictions is the strongest, gather together all of its anti-
> dotes and subdue that affliction first.

Then you will be free of any obstacles to the meditation.

> **Abandon all hope of results.**
>
> As you practice lojong, you should abandon all self-cen-
> tered desires such as wishing for wealth and honor in
> this life, the happiness of the gods or humans in the
> next, or wanting to attain nirvana for yourself alone.

Of course this commentary is good: this is the right way. But *abandon all hope of results* also means that when you are in meditation, you should not be so hungry for good results. Simply, if you are expecting your meditation to achieve some specific result, that will delay everything and cause stress in the mind. Hope and doubt about whether you are doing it right or wrong are disturbing thoughts that will contaminate your meditation.

> **Avoid poisoned food.**
>
> Mixing any virtuous practice with the assumption that
> things actually exist and self-cherishing is like mixing
> food with poison, so give it up.

Of course, most of the believers in karma will go for this idea that you do something good for a good return. That's okay, but for lojong practice it is not the right attitude. Of course, if you do something good for your own benefit, it is better than not doing anything good at all. But lojong is a very highly-qualified practice so this kind of attitude does not match with it. *Avoid poisoned food* means that any calculating [the scope of benefit] is not for yourself but is one hundred per cent for sentient beings.

> **Do not make a point of constancy**.
>
> Do not harbor resentment.

Yeah, that translation is correct; in Tibetan it is quite confusing. A common meaning of these words is that if someone helps you, you should not forget it; you should always appreciate the other's kindness. So here it says, don't do that. It doesn't explain it clearly here. The commentary just says *do not harbor resentment*, which for the English reader is okay. But for Tibetans and many other people, there is a tendency to misinterpret this. In Tibetan we have a saying, "Take note of others' kindness." This also refers to being resentful of those who harm you—it's moralistic advice. If someone helps you, you should be helpful back and if someone harms you don't just accept it—you must take revenge, they say. This may be good for kings or ministers or generals, but it's not good for Dharma or lojong practice. Don't be like that.

> **Avoid the agitation of hurtful talk**.
>
> Do not answer others' insults with harsh repartees. Do not uncaringly call attention to others' transgressions.

This means that if somebody says or does something bad to you, you may keep it and wait for an opportunity to take revenge. Don't do that! [*laughter*]

> **Do not wait in ambush**.
>
> When others have hurt you, you might keep it hidden in your heart until the time for revenge is nigh. Give it up.

Do not focus on others' sore points.

Do not expose people's hidden faults. Nor should you misuse the life-mantras of non-humans or use other methods which may cause great damage to others' minds.

All of these are the usual habits of crafty, cunning humans, aren't they?

Do not burden a cow with an ox's load.

When saddled with an unwelcome duty or reprimand, do not try to cheat and pass it on to others so that they become the patsy.

Do not try to divert responsibilities which others may find difficult. Many crafty people, many politicians do that. [*laughter*] It's so easy.

Do not play to win.

Do not use different techniques to acquire collective resources for your private enjoyment.

It's like property owners in early times—they often got hold of their land in this way. Not all the time, but quite often. Through encroachment.

Do not misuse magic.

Do not try to bolster your self-image by taking defeat upon yourself or practicing lojong like a magic ceremony in order to pacify demons, malevolent forces, or maladies.

Lojong is not about rituals; it should not be used like a ritual to gain popularity. Some good lojong practitioners are really able to relieve others' pain by doing tonglen. It can be done. Of course, you should help sentient beings—but don't advertise too much that you are good at it. Otherwise you will become like those ritual lamas in Tibet who go door-to-door offering rituals. Their minds are totally distracted because, in fact, they want to collect wealth. Don't use lojong practice for that kind of activity.

> **Do not turn a god into a demon**.
> If the practice of lojong has reinforced your pride and arrogance, then the practice has not been effective and is Dharma no longer.

You have to be your own witness and see whether your pride has become bigger or not. If someone accuses you of being a fake lojong practitioner or a fake teacher, check whether you are hurt by that or not, if you become more angry or not. Instead of focusing on whether you have attained some miracle powers, test yourself to see whether your pride is increasing or decreasing. It is very important to test yourself. If your pride has increased, there is no point in claiming that you are a lojong practitioner.

> It is as senseless as trying to placate an evil spirit of the east by sending compensation to the west.

Tibetan nomads have these kinds of proverbs. A lot of nomadic proverbs are used here in order to make the meaning clear to them.

> Accordingly, having abandoned vanity and self-cherishing, be everyone's most humble servant.

Do not look to make pain part of pleasure.

This is easy to understand.

"If my friends or Dharma brethren were to die, their food, money, texts, and shrine objects would be mine."

That's only for lamas, not for you.

"If my benefactor were struck by a fatal illness, I would receive plenty of offerings. If a great meditator of my league were to die, his wealth and influence would become mine alone. If my enemy were to die, no one would bother me and that would make me happy . . . ." Thoughts such as these—the desire that others might suffer so as to ensure your own pleasure—must be rejected.

If a very dangerous enemy of the world were to die, as a lojong practitioner I would be happy because the evil one could not fulfill his bad wishes and people would be safe from his harm. So my attitude is not wrong. Otherwise, if anything is being calculated for your own benefit, then it's wrong. You have to carefully analyze your attitude in this way.

We'll take a break now and start again after lunch.

Session 4

The **seventh point** presents **mind training guidelines**.
There is one way to do all practices.

Everything you do, including practices involving food, clothing, and so on, should benefit others.

For example, in his book the *Bodhicharyavatara*, Shantideva says a lot about what you should be thinking when you are eating, and how you should dedicate it for all sentient beings.

Confront all problems with one solution.

When faced with illness, demons, evil spirits, and people's hatred, if you do not genuinely wish to apply mind training to the situation even though you have been practicing lojong, think: "Most living beings are in the same boat. May their faults dissolve into me."

This means thinking that many other practitioners who are not successful face the same kinds of problems that I am facing now, so all of their faults and mistakes should be absorbed by me. Instead of regretting that you are not successful because of these obstacles, use them to make the wish that others' problems will be absorbed into your own so that they can be freed from theirs. Then, instead of the problems disturbing you, more merit will be created—three times, a thousand times more merit.

> **In the beginning, in the end: two things to do.**
> At the start of the morning, think with great determina-tion: "Today I shall not be separated from the two bo-dhicittas." In the evening as you go to sleep, consider the day's activities and make a list of all the misdoings that went against bodhicitta. Acknowledge them and make sure they will not happen again.

Wow! One Kadampa lineage holder—I think it was Lan-gri Thangpa—was always very aware of what was going on in his mind. He kept many black and white stones and whenever evil thoughts arose, he would pick up a black stone and place it like so [creating a small heap]. And when he could implement the mind training meth-od, he would add a white stone instead. In the begin-ning, most of the time there were black stones and very, very few white. Then, gradually, the white increased. Fi-nally, later, there were no black stones, only white ones. He tested himself in this way. For you, instead of using a pen and notebook [to chart your progress], maybe you can use your mobile phone for that. [*laughter*]

> **Patiently accept whichever of the two occurs**.
> Even if you have wealth, power, attendants, and pros-

> perity, do not be proud, but recognize them as an illu-
> sion. And even if everything falls apart and you have
> sunk so low that water is all you have left, think of it as
> an illusion and practice tonglen. Be neither arrogant nor
> despondent.

You can understand this easily. It is useful to apply the concept of impermanence and remember that all things are like a mirage. If you do, they will not bother you. In relative truth, why should you be disappointed? Why should you be overly expectant and excited? Everything is changing anyway and you will have to leave it all behind. Nothing will follow you forever, so there is no point in being proud when you have it and no point in being disappointed when you miss it. On the basis of the view of absolute truth, nothing is really existent: it's just a mirage. Remembering this, don't cling to anything.

> **Keep both as if your life depended on it**.
> Guard the general Dharma precepts and the specific
> lojong vows as you guard your life.

Since you are fully aware, this is the key to the meaning of life and the solution for enlightenment. You are already on the path to enlightenment, so why not keep these precepts as if they were as precious as your life—or even more.

> **Train in the three challenges**.
> When negative emotions arise, the first challenge is to
> be aware of them, the next is to keep them at bay, and
> the last is to finish them off. As for the first, recognize
> them as soon as they surface.

If you have already become good at using the realization of the mind-nature view on every affliction, then you will not be bothered by these negative emotions. If you are not good at that practice, then you should maintain awareness. You should be very careful about afflictions because if you don't suppress them at the beginning, then once they arise, they will keep escalating. They will multiply and will be difficult to subdue. It is very easy to subdue them in the beginning, so you should try to recognize them immediately.

> Next, use remedies to dispose of them. Finally, apply whichever methods will keep them from arising in the future.

Once you can recognize and stop them, then it is very easy to prevent them from arising again.

> **Adopt the three principle causes**.
> Adopt these three: meeting with an excellent lama, . . .

This means meeting with an excellent spiritual teacher or excellent Buddhist teacher: an excellent bodhisattva teacher.

> . . . practicing the Dharma with a compliant mind, . . .

This means workable: your mind should be well-trained so it is easy to use it for practice.

> . . . and gathering appropriate conditions for practice.

The Buddha organized the vinaya for his disciples so that they could gather the appropriate conditions for practice. His disciples were not involved in worldly life—they were completely free from worldly life because they wanted to practice meditation for seventeen or eighteen hours a day. They slept from about ten o'clock at night to three or four in the morning; otherwise they were meditating.

They had to get food, so the Buddha allowed them to beg for food. He created rules of conduct so that his disciples would not behave like pushy beggars and disturb the peace of the people. He chose a uniform for easy identification and had his monks walk gently to let people know that they were there for food. If in one area they had nothing to give, the monks would not stay; they would walk away gently and go somewhere else where people were able to offer something. Once the monks got their food, they would go back to the temple.

The Buddha organized many rules of conduct in order to prevent his monastics from being greedy, or misbehaving, and so forth. The goal of all these rules was to make practice successful. Not eating after 1 p.m. helps practitioners to avoid falling asleep and keeps the mind clear—and also it is cheaper! [*laughter*] So, there were many good ideas that contributed to good and appropriate conditions for practice.

Unfailingly cultivate three things.

Unfailingly observe devotion, mind training and the rules of moral conduct, including the most minor ones.

With devotion, you can draw the blessings of the great bodhisattvas. They have all dedicated a lot of meritorious activity for the good of their disciples and sentient beings; if you have clear devotion, you can receive their blessings. Your devotion will cooperate with their dedications of merit.

As I explained, mind training and the rules of moral conduct encompass monks' and laymen's conduct. All advice given by the Buddha is very practical. It is not bound by religion. All forms of conduct taught in Dharma are free from religion, except Vajrayana. But if you adopt the deep view, Vajrayana is not bound by religion either, even if superficially it is. The practices of Mahayana and Theravada are completely free from religion. They are not religious. Their rules of conduct exist according to practitioners' needs.

The *Bodhicharyavatara* teaches how to keep proper conduct, but it isn't religious—it follows nature. For example, it advises: be gentle, do not be involved so much in society or you may be influenced by others' problems, and don't be unfriendly. This is all normal behavior, like when the Buddha recommended that young meditators who fetched water from a well should use a bronze ladle so that they could see the bugs. It was good for health and good to prevent killing bugs: natural conduct.

So the conduct recommended in the Dharma, the Buddha's teachings, is not bound by the concept of religion. My understanding is that in some religions, people keep the precepts so that gods or deities will favor them. Like, for instance, Brahmins and Kriyatantra practitioners who follow Brahmin precepts like not eating garlic because if they do, the Brahmin deity will not come to them. Therefore, they do not eat garlic. These are religious precepts.

In lojong, conduct is bound by karma and normal concepts. You should not behave against society's standards, like being a thief, or going naked and embarrassing everybody. Tattoos—I don't know. Tattoos are quite rare, aren't they? Well, it's probably a superstition, but many Tibetan adults say that if you paint yourself, you will not be successful in business. So too many tattoos are not advisable for many reasons and that is one of them. What do you think? Are tattoos necessary for society? Not necessary. [*chuckling*] I know one young man who has a Chenrezig tattoo on his back and now he does not know how to sleep. [*much laughter*]

> **Make sure you have the inseparable three**.
> Never separate the body, speech, and mind from virtue.
>
> **Train impartially in every instance. Once deep and inclusive training has taken place, love everyone**.
> Train wholeheartedly, not just rhetorically. Encompass all living beings in your training.

Motivation. Train your heart to have love for all sentient beings. You're not just following tradition, not just pretending, not just doing it to impress people. You, yourself, must be the witness as to whether you really have genuine love or not. Train your mind and your heart to have genuine love towards all sentient beings.

> **Always practice with special cases**.
> Your companions and rivals; those far removed who have not harmed you and those close by who have; those whom you instinctively dislike because of karma, and so on: make these difficult cases the special object of your practice.

When you are facing all these difficulties, you implement the practice even more. Then these special cases will be an additional condition that you can use for increasing the power of your practice.

> **Do not concern yourself with external circumstances**.

Do not concern yourself with whether or not there is an abundance of food and clothing; whether or not there is suffering; whether your lodgings are pleasant or un-pleasant; whether your health is good or bad, and so forth.

Put the most important things into practice now.

Thus far, taking rebirth in samsara has been senseless; the time has come to accomplish the most important things. These are the Dharma, which is more important than any goals related to this lifetime; actual practice, which is more important than learning; and bodhicitta, which is more important than any other spiritual achievement. Therefore, put these into practice.

Without practice, just learning Buddhism will not help you. You must use what you've learned: you must practice. The solution to life, the meaning of life, is knowing the practice of Dharma, including the details. But if you're just spinning around in the learning part only, then you are wasting your life by not putting your knowledge to use. Therefore, practice.

Do not misconstrue.

Misguided patience is being unable to bear suffering connected with Dharma practice, but able to bear everyday worldly suffering.

This is very true. Most people can tolerate worldly suffering, worldly difficulties that are more difficult than when you are in meditation, but not difficulties related to Dharma practice. That's because of craving and self-clinging to your physical form.

Misguided resolve is lacking the aspiration to practice Dharma, but aspiring to carry out activities connected to this life.

They say that Confucius was very practical. However, his followers recommend that you think more about this life than the next because if you don't know what is good for this life, why think about the next one? I disagree—that logic is not very accurate. In my opinion, thinking about the next life is excellent.

> Misguided taste is not having a taste for the Dharma, but having a taste for the things of this world.

Yes, this is also misguided. No one has achieved ultimate happiness by craving this life, enjoying this life. No one has ever achieved ultimate enjoyment from this [samsaric] life. The richest people have constant suffering, and prominent politicians also have so much suffering. Good meditators who enjoy meditating day and night are the only ones who achieve ultimate happiness. Even when their conditions are totally uncomfortable and they are sleeping in caves where there are scorpions, their minds are very happy. Of course, physically they have to be free from scorpions biting, but mentally they enjoy life because ultimate happiness develops in the mind.

You can never be bored with ultimate happiness because it is true happiness. If your happiness is artificial, then you can become bored and will no longer be happy with it. Meditation experience will transform your stream of mind so that there is no longer room for unhappiness. Someone who does not understand this is misguided.

> Misguided compassion is not practicing compassion towards wrongdoers, but fostering compassion for those who practice austerities in the name of Dharma.

When Milarepa was meditating in the cave without clothes, his sister came and said, "We are the last [most miserable] humans in this world," which meant, "What you are doing is crazy. You don't even have clothes to wear and you are singing in the cave. What are you doing?" She was expressing pity, no? Here this means don't feel pity for the great practitioners.

When the lamas came from Tibet, they didn't know any languages other than Tibetan. The Nepalese people in Sikkim and Nepal felt so much pity—they were thinking, "These lamas don't know anything about how to live." They described them with words which meant "worthy of pity." But the lamas did know how to live— they were enjoying meditation! The lamas who went to jail because they didn't have passports didn't want to come back out! [*laughter*] Many of them tried to stay. After one lama came out of the Sikkim jail, he broke someone's window just so he could go back in. [*laughter*] They could meditate in prison—there was enough food for prisoners there, and they enjoyed that.

> Misguided caring is not encouraging those who depend upon us to engage in Dharma-related activities, but encouraging them to do worldly activities.
>
> Misguided rejoicing is not being delighted when others find happiness and joy, but jubilating when enemies experience suffering.

These are easy to understand.

> Having rejected the six misconstrued points, practice the six correct ones.
>
> **Do not be inconsistent**.
>
> When conviction in the Dharma fails to develop, some-

> times you practice and sometimes you do not. Aban-
> doning this pattern, uninterruptedly and one-pointedly
> engage in mind training.

Like the story of Asanga who was practicing day and
night in a cave for many years, praying to meet [his meditation deity] Maitreya Buddha face to face. He eventually decided to leave his practice because he had had
no success. After three years he went out, and he met
a lady who was sharpening a knife with a feather. He
said to her, "How is it that by sharpening a knife with a
feather it could become much sharper than others?" She
answered, "It is because of diligence. With consistency,
I can sharpen this knife very well with a feather." Then
he understood, "Oh, this is a lesson for me," and he went
back to practice for another three years.

Again, Asanga felt that he wasn't achieving anything
and went out of his cave. Again, he met a person; this
one was rubbing a cloth on a boulder. "What are you doing?" he asked. "I want to reduce the height of the rock,"
the man replied. "How can you do that?" Asanga won-
dered. "I can do it by rubbing it with a cloth. You can do
anything if you have diligence." Then Asanga went back
and did three more years of practice.

When he left the cave again, he met a dog that was
wounded and maggots were moving around in the
wound. Suddenly, strong compassion rose up in him.
He wanted to remove the worms, but if he did so with
a stick he might harm them, so he decided to lick them
out with his tongue. At the very moment his tongue was
about to touch the maggots, the wounded dog was no
longer there, and Maitreya Buddha appeared.

What does this mean? When the mind is finally
shining, finally ready, the remedy appears as a wound-

ed dog. Actually, this was Asanga's illusion, but *this* illusion was the antidote. When his mind was cleansed of karmic influences, the remedy appeared as a wounded dog, and this caused enormous compassion to rise up. Asanga did not hesitate to try to remove the worms with his tongue—very, very dirty worms. Then he could see Maitreya Buddha and receive all of his instructions.

Asanga asked Maitreya why others didn't see him. Maitreya explained that it was because of their karmic obscurations. To demonstrate this, Maitreya Buddha sat on Asanga's shoulder and they went into town. The people there didn't see anything, except for one old lady who saw that he was carrying a dead dog. "Why are you carrying a dead dog?" she asked. This means that the old lady was also special—she had a special rebirth which is called "impure but pure." The rest of the people were totally impure so they couldn't see anything.

Diligence is necessary. Whether you are successful or not, you should not be disappointed. Be like the tortoise when racing with the hare. Do you know that story? A tortoise and a hare were racing, and at the end the rabbit was behind and the tortoise was already at the finish because he had continued on with diligence.

> **Practice decisively.**
> Once your mind has completely surrendered to mind training, make it your only practice.

One should not be gullible—is that the right word? Like when you hear something convincing and then immediately follow that new practice. You change practices.

For example, people who are influenced by marketing might change their medicines. So when people get sick, many of them use all kinds of medicine that are commercialized. Nothing works for them because they are not consistently using one remedy. One medicine today and another medicine tomorrow: not so effective. Generally, when you follow one medical treatment, you should completely rely on it. Unless the treatment is wrong, you will be treated; you will be helped.

Like Angulimala,[8] who went in the wrong direction and started killing people. He killed nine hundred and ninety-nine people and achieved nothing. He met the Buddha, stopped killing and did practice, and he became an arhat.

Practice is like this. With lojong or any other practice, once you've learned how to do it well, you should completely rely on it. Of course you have to find the right practice. Once you have found it, completely rely on it, like Asanga did during all those years. Then you will achieve the result.

Free yourself by examining and analyzing.

Assess which disturbing emotion dominates your mindstream and make an earnest effort to eliminate it.

That's the same as *Purify whichever affliction is strongest first.* Implement the view on the affliction to eliminate it.

Do not make a habit of showing off.

Do not boast about being kind to someone; or practic-

---

8   Angulimala—He of the Fingerbone Garland—was a contemporary of the Buddha's whose story is told in the sutras. His teacher, in whom he had the utmost confidence, told Angulimala that in order to conclude his spiritual training, he was to bring him a thousand fingerbones. Angulimala, devoted and perturbed, set off on a killing spree. He had almost reached his goal when he met the Buddha and had a radical change of heart.

> ing the Dharma for a long time; or being a scholar or
> renunciant, and so on.

Do not boast by saying, "I have done a lot of practice, so why don't you appreciate me? Why don't you respect me? I am such a renounced person!" What's that? That's being very angry that people don't appreciate how I'm doing the practice. That can happen. A kind of naive practitioner can do that.

> **Do not be irritable**.
> Do not become irritated if, for example, someone of-
> fends you in public.

That's simple.

> **Do not be capricious**.
> Avoid openly expressing your approval or disapproval of
> every little thing which occurs.

Also simple.

> **Do not crave thanks**.
> Do not crave the prestige of being thanked if, for in-
> stance, you have helped others.

Do not crave the prestige of being thanked for showing compassion or generosity. Do not try to earn prestige.

All right. The seven points are finished.

> *Belonging to the transmission of Serlingpa,*
> *this is the essence of the elixir of the pith instructions.*
> *When the five degenerations are gaining ground,*

| *it transforms them into the path of awakening.* |

The entire practice is for this: transforming the five degenerations—time, living beings, lifespan, emotional afflictions, and views—into the path. All of the practice methods, as well as the conduct and advice, are there so that you can use all circumstances and experiences—bad and good—to practice.

In this way, you are totally free from obstacles. Bad is okay, you know how to use it for practice. Good, of course, is okay too. Therefore everything provides causes and conditions for your practice.

> [This is the Elixir of Dharma which transforms the five degenerations—time, living beings, lifespan, emotional afflictions, and view—into the path.]
>
> *When karmic tendencies due to past training were rekindled,*
> *I was so deeply inspired that it led me to request*
> *—with utter disregard for suffering and defamation—*
> *the oral instructions which subdue self-clinging.*
> *Were I to die this instant, I would have no regrets.*

That's what Spiritual Friend Chekawa said at the time. After he became enlightened, he composed these words. He had some tea and gave tea to his disciples, and they celebrated the seven points of mind training. Since that time, this lineage has been passed on from teachers to disciples.

> Spiritual Friend Chekawa expresses his absolute confidence in this Dharma teaching with these words. If there is just one kind of Dharma to be practiced, it should be this. This concise explanation of the practice was composed by the fifth Shamarpa.

The fifth Shamarpa composed this commentary, and it is no different from others like the one by Ngulchu Thogmé, for example. They are the same. Thank you for your patience with my instructions.

Glossary

Amitabha (literally "Limitless Light") The name of the buddha who presides over the buddha realm of *Sukhavati*.

Arhat A noble one who has subdued disturbing emotions by following the Hinayana teachings and has attained "cessation," or nirvana. The last of four stages of realization, it is preceded by the stages of stream-entrant, once-returner, and non-returner.

Asanga (c. 290–350 C.E.) The founder of the *cittamatra* system of tenets. In this system, based upon such sutras as the *Lankavatara* and *Dashabhumika* sutras, all phenomena are asserted to be "merely mind" and hence the system's designation as "mind only" (Skt. *cittamatra*). Both Asanga and his half-brother Vasubandhu authored a number of works setting out this philosophy.

Bardo (literally "transition") A term that refers here to the state between death and rebirth. Although it was described in the *Abhidharma*, the most detailed presentation of the nature of the bardo and the opportunities it affords for liberation is found in the tantras.

Bhumi (literally "ground" or "level") This term signifies the stages of spiritual achievement through which bodhisattvas pass on the Mahayana path to Buddhahood. They are divided into two parts: the stages of ordinary practitioners and the stages of "noble ones" who, having attained non-dual primordial wisdom, have decisively cut their connection with samsara. There are ten successive levels traversed by the "noble" bodhisattvas or Mahayana practitioners. The first seven are said to be "impure" while the last three are termed "pure," since the obscurations of disturbing emotions and incomplete knowledge have been removed. Only the most subtle obscurations remain to be dispelled.

Bodhicitta Both the compassionate motivation of a bodhisattva and the wisdom mind of such a being. The presence of motivation and wisdom is the *sine qua non* of Mahayana, the Great Vehicle. The two aspects are referred to as conventional and ultimate bodhicitta respectively.

Bodhisattva Anyone who has taken the vow to attain buddhahood for the benefit of all sentient beings (i.e. the bodhisattva vow). Sometimes the term is used specifically in reference to "noble" bodhisattvas, i.e. those who have attained the bhumis. Bodhisattvas have, through taking the vow, engendered bodhicitta, which they seek to stabilize and increase by putting the mind training and other instructions into practice.

Bodhisattvayana (literally "bodhisattva vehicle") in this usage is synonymous with "Mahayana."

Chenrezig The bodhisattva who embodies the power of awakened compassion. In the Mahayana, he is referred to as one of the "eight sons of the Buddha." Chenrezig is also one of the four major Vajrayana deities practiced in the Kadam tradition.

Chöd The *Chöd* (literally "severance") tradition originated with the Indian Dampa Sanjay (d. 1117) and his Tibetan disciples, Kyo Sönam Lama and the yogini Machik Labdrön (1055–1149). Through meditating on emptiness and offering their bodies to all sentient beings, especially beings of a demonic nature, Chöd practitioners perfect generosity and sever attachment to the notion of a truly existent self. The practice of Chöd has been maintained in the Kagyu and Nyingma traditions and, to a lesser extent, within the Gelug tradition.

Dorjé Sempa The meditation deity who embodies the primordial purity of mind and whose liturgy and meditation are practiced to purify non-virtuous actions, especially lapses of vows.

Dromtönpa (1005–1064) The principal Tibetan disciple

of Atisha and founder of Reting, the first monastic establishment of the Kadam tradition.

Genyen(ma) The first of the three principal types of "individual liberation" (Skt. *pratimoksha*) vow and the only one available to householders; the other two are reserved for monastics. The genyen discipline in full has five rules of training.

Gélong(ma) A fully ordained monastic holder of the "individual liberation" vow. In the *Mula-Sarvastivada* tradition of the vinaya, to which all schools of Tibetan Buddhism adhere, the fully ordained monk observes 265 rules and the fully ordained nun 360.

Gétsul(ma) A novice monastic, male or female, whose "individual liberation" vow is less detailed than that of the gélong, comprising only 36 rules of training for monks as well as for nuns.

Hinayana (literally "the Lesser Vehicle;" sometimes *Shravakayana*, "the Vehicle of the Disciples") is the term used in *Mahayana* scriptures to designate the spiritual aims and practices of those who follow the Buddhist path in order to dispel the causes of suffering within their own individual streams of being. In contrast, the aim of the Mahayana system is to achieve Buddhahood for the benefit of all beings.

Nowadays the term *Theravada* ("Doctrine of the Elders") has found favor in place of the potentially pejorative "Hinayana." However, although there is much in common between the tenets and disciplines of Theravada and other Shravakayana schools, it should be noted that there was a flourishing Mahayana culture within Theravada in Sri Lanka in the medieval period. This reflects the fact that Theravada is essentially a transmission of the codes of monastic discipline and can therefore support Mahayana spiritual practice.

Kadam The Kadam school was established by Dromtön in the 11th century. The name itself signifies "Those bound by the word" (i.e. of the Buddha). In later centuries, the Kadam teachings had been largely absorbed by the Kagyu and Gelug schools and had ceased to exist as an independent lineage.

Kagyu The Kagyu tradition began in Tibet with Marpa Lotsawa (1012–1097) who unified in himself two major streams of "tantra in one lineage:" the "close" and "distant" lineages received from Naropa and Maitripa, respectively. The two succeeding patriarchs of the tradition were Milarepa (1040–1123) and Gampopa (1079–1153). It was the latter who blended the tantric teachings of his predecessors Marpa and Milarepa with the largely sutra-oriented teachings of the Kadam school, giving the Kagyu tradition its distinctive and enduring characteristics.

Kalachakra A tantra of the non-dual *anuttarayoga* class. It was brought to India from the mystical kingdom of Shambhala by the yogin Chilupa and subsequently popularized in Tibet by masters such as Dolpopa Sherab Gyaltsen (1292–1361).

Kathog Rigzin Chenpo a.k.a. Rigzin Tséwang Norbu (1698-1755) A highly influential Nyingma master from the monastery of Katok in eastern Tibet who held both the lojong and *zhentong* ("extrinsic emptiness") lineages.

Kaya The Sanskrit term *kaya* refers to the "bodies" or, perhaps, modalities of a buddha. As such, the *dharmakaya* ("body of truth") signifies the ultimate modality of a buddha, which possesses a two-fold purity: that of the intrinsically pure nature of mind, existent in all beings; and that unique to buddhas, which arises through the purification of obscurations that currently veil the natural purity of mind. This purification is brought about by the development of primordial wisdom which correctly discerns the nature of all "dharmas" (phenomena), giving the term "dharmakaya."

As the dharmakaya transcends all dualistic elaborations, it is imperceptible to all except fully enlightened beings. Therefore, a buddha's liberating activity for others is carried out through the *sambhogakaya* ("body of enjoyment") and *nirmanakaya* ("body of transformation").

Sambhogakaya possesses the "five certainties" of form, realm, disciples, duration, and teaching, and manifests only to bodhisattvas of the highest spiritual level. Nirmanakaya can be perceived by ordinary beings and communicates the Dharma both directly and indirectly. Thus a "supreme nirmanakaya," such as Buddha Shakyamuni, can appear in this ordinary world and enact the twelve great deeds, including taking birth, attaining enlightenment, teaching, and passing away. "Birth nirmanakaya" appears in a variety of forms—human and even animal—and "art nirmanakaya" communicates the Dharma through various art forms.

The fourth kaya is termed the *svabhavikakaya* ("integral body"). It signifies the essential unity of the above three modalities, since the three kayas are neither one nor different.

Kriya Tantra The first of the four sets of tantra, the Kriya (Skt. for "activity") tantras place great emphasis on techniques involving ritual activity and purity.

Langri Thangpa (1054–1123) The author of "The Eight Verses of Mind Training" and one of the most famous early masters of the Kadam tradition.

Lojong Lojong (literally "mind training") is a special system of meditation on bodhicitta that was introduced in Tibet by Atisha in the 11th century. Transmitted by the early Kadampa masters, lojong was subsequently preserved in all four of the major traditions of Buddhism in Tibet.

Madhyamaka The Middle Way view is the philosophical system founded by Nagarjuna on the basis of the *Perfection of Wisdom* sutras. In madhyamaka the two philosophical extremes of "eternalism" and "annihilationism" are rejected in the recognition that the nature of reality transcends all conceptual and linguistic designations.

Mahamudra (literally "The Great Seal") In the new tantra schools of Kagyu, Sakya and Gelug, mahamudra signifies the realization of primordial wisdom attained through the unification of the development and completion stages of anuttarayoga tantra.

Mahayana (literally "The Great Vehicle") The path practiced by bodhisattvas. The objective of its followers, as defined by the Buddha in the extensive Mahayana sutras, is to become a buddha in order to benefit all beings rather than to attain freedom from suffering for oneself alone, which is understood to be the objective of those following the Hinayana (literally "The Lesser Vehicle").

Maitreya The regent of Shakyamuni Buddha, Maitreya currently dwells in the divine realm of Tushita. After the final disappearance of the doctrine of Shakyamuni (the 4th buddha of this cycle), he will appear in this world as the 5th buddha of this cycle and reveal the Dharma.

Manjushri The bodhisattva who embodies the awakened wisdom of enlightenment. Many forms of Manjushri have been delineated in the tantras, and meditation upon this tutelary deity is popular in all schools of Tibetan Buddhism.

Milarepa (1040–1123) Consummate Vajrayana master and poet who was the second of the three founding fathers of the Kagyu tradition.

Nagarjuna (c. 1st century CE) One of the greatest thinkers in Buddhist history and founder of the Madhyamaka system of tenets. Author of a variety of influential works such as the *Root Verses on the Middle Way* and *Letter to a Friend*. His principal disciple was Aryadeva.

Paramita The term *paramita* (commonly translated as "perfection") refers to the six principal practices of a bodhisattva: generous giving, moral discipline, patience, effort, meditation or concentration, and wisdom. According to the common teachings of the Mahayana, it is by perfecting these qualities that the journey to buddhahood is accomplished.

Potowa or **Potawa** (1027–1105) One of the so-called "Three Cousins," alongside Phuchungwa and Chen-ngawa. The three key disciples of Dromtön, they were highly influential in the early history of the Kadam tradition. Potowa's chief disciples were Sharawa and Langri Thangpa.

Powa or **Phowa** In general the term *powa* refers to the anuttarayoga tantra practice by which the yogin or yogini achieves the transference of their consciousness to the "pure lands," thus circumventing rebirth in the bardo after having died. There is also a distinctly Mahayana form of the practice in the lojong cycle of instructions.

Samsara The mode of being, dependent upon ignorance and disturbing emotions and characterized by suffering, within which all beings cycle until it has been brought to an end in nirvana.

Samantabhadra As one of the "eight close sons" of the Buddha, Samantabhadra is one of the chief Mahayana bodhisattvas. The aspirational prayer associated with this bodhisattva is amongst the most popular Mahayana liturgies.

Sangha The Sangha (literally "community") is the third of the Three Jewels, alongside the Buddha and Dharma. In the Mahayana, the sangha consists of both the ordained sangha and the householder sangha.

Sharawa (1070–1141) An early Kadampa master who, as a disciple of Géshé Potowa, transmitted the lojong teaching to Géshé Chekawa.

Shiné Calm Abiding meditation. A meditation technique that enables a state of calmness, stability and focused attentiveness and thus serves as an essential prerequisite for the practice of *lhaktong*, or insight.

Sugata (literally the "one gone to bliss") An epithet for the Buddha.

Sutra The term "sutra" designates a general Dharma discourse given by the Buddha. In a wider context it refers to the teachings of the Three Baskets, comprising sutra, abhidharma and vinaya, as opposed to the teachings of "tantra," taken here to signify the totality of the Vajrayana teaching.

Tantra Scriptures presenting the esoteric "uncommon Mahayana": the Vajrayana teachings of the Buddha. According to most Indian and Tibetan masters, the tantras can be grouped in four sets: kriya, charya, yoga, and anuttara yoga.

Within the Buddhist canon, it is most appropriate to regard them as constituting a fourth "basket," or collection, of the Buddha's teaching alongside the sutra, abhidharma, and vinaya collections.

Theravada See Hinayana.

Tonglen (literally "sending and taking") The key meditational practice within the lojong system. When practicing tonglen one exchanges one's own happiness and virtues for the suffering and non-virtues of others, thus striving to achieve others' welfare and strengthen one's bodhicitta.

Torma Generally, a torma is a type of offering sculpted from flour and butter and used in rituals connected with Vajrayana deities.
In the context of mind training, tormas are used as offerings to various types of deities who protect the transmission of the teachings, and as a placatory gift to spirits.

Vajrayana The uncommon Mahayana path based on instructions transmitted in the tantras. Due to its exceptional skillful means, such as the esoteric practices of initiation and deity yoga, Vajrayana potentially leads more swiftly to buddhahood than the "common" Mahayana path as set out in the sutras.

Vajrayogini One of the principal meditation deities of the anuttarayoga tantra, Vajrayogini belongs in the *Chakrasamvara* cycle of tantras. Consequently, she has played a central role in the spiritual curriculums of both the Kagyu and Sakya schools of Tibet.

The **Vinaya** is the collection of the Buddha's teachings on moral training. It forms one of the Three Baskets of his teaching, alongside the sutra and abhidharma collections.

Yogachara The Mahayana system of tenets also known as the *cittamatra*, or Mind Only, school of Buddhist philosophy.

As presented in the book	This word is a	Sanskrit spelling with diacritics	Tibetan Wylie spelling
Amitabha	Sanskrit name	Amitābha	'od dpag med
arhat	Sanskrit term	arhat	dgra bcom pa
bardo	Tibetan term	antarābhava	bar do
bhumi	Sanskrit term	bhūmi	sa
bodhicitta	Sanskrit term	bodhicitta	byang chub kyi sems
bodhisattva	Sanskrit term	bodhisattva	byang chub sems dpa'
Bodhisattvayana	Sanskrit term	Bodhisattvayāna	byang chub sems dpa'i theg pa
Chenrezig	Tibetan name	Avalokiteśvara	spyan ras gzigs
chöd	Tibetan term	--	gcod
Dorjé Sempa	Tibetan name	Vajrasattva	rdo rje sems dpa'
Dromtönpa	Tibetan name	--	'brom ston pa
genyen(ma)	Tibetan term	upāsaka/upāsikā	dge bsnyen (ma)
gélong(ma)	Tibetan term	bhikṣu/bhikṣuṇī	dge slong (ma)

gétsul(ma)	Tibetan term	śrāmaṇera/ śrāmaṇerikā	dge tshul (ma)
Hinayana	Sanskrit term	Hīnayāna	theg dman
Kadam	Tibetan term	--	bka' gdams
Kagyu	Tibetan term	--	bka' brgyud
Kalachakra	Sanskrit term	Kālacakra	dus kyi 'khor lo
Kathog Rigzin Chenpo	Tibetan name	--	kaH thog rig 'dzin chen po
kaya	Sanskrit term	kāya	sku
Kriya tantra	Sanskrit term	Kriyātantra	bya rgyud
Langri Thangpa	Tibetan name	--	glang ri thang pa
lhaktong	Tibetan term	vipaśyanā	lhag mthong
lojong	Tibetan term	--	blo sbyong
Madhyamaka	Sanskrit term	Madhyamaka	dbu ma
Mahamudra	Sanskrit term	Mahāmudrā	phyag rgya chen po
Mahayana	Sanskrit term	Mahāyāna	theg pa chen po

Maitreya	Sanskrit name	Maitreya	*byams pa*
Manjushri	Sanskrit name	Mañjuśrī	*'jam dpal dbyang*
Milarepa	Tibetan name	--	*mi la ras pa*
Nagarjuna	Sanskrit name	Nāgārjuna	*klu sgrub*
paramita	Sanskrit term	pāramitā	*pha rol tu phyin pa*
Potowa/Potawa	Tibetan name	--	*po to ba*
powa/phowa	Tibetan term	--	*'pho ba*
samsara	Sanskrit term	saṃsāra	*'khor ba*
Samantabhadra	Sanskrit name	Samantabhadra	*kun tu bzang po*
Sangha	Sanskrit term	Saṅgha	*dge 'dun*
Sharawa	Tibetan name	--	*sha ra ba*
shiné	Tibetan term	śamatha	*zhi gnas*
sugata	Sanskrit term	sugata	*bde bar gshegs pa*
sutra	Sanskrit term	sūtra	*mdo*

tantra	Sanskrit term	tantra	*rgyud*
tonglen	Tibetan term	--	*gtong len*
torma	Tibetan term	bali	*gtor ma*
Vajrayana	Sanskrit term	Vajrayāna	*rdo rje theg pu*
Vajrayogini	Sanskrit name	Vajrayoginī	*rdo rje rnal 'byor ma*
Vinaya	Sanskrit term	Vinaya	*'dul ba*
Yogachara	Sanskrit term	Yogācāra	*rnal 'byor gyi spyod*

About the Author

Shamar Rinpoche, Mipham Chökyi Lodrö (1952–2014), was the 14th Shamarpa. The Shamarpa or "Red Hat Lama of Tibet" is Tibetan Buddhism's second oldest reincarnate lineage after the Karmapa lineage. Born in Derge, Tibet, Shamar Rinpoche was recognized by the 16th Gyalwa Karmapa in 1957 and was enthroned as the 14th Shamarpa in 1963. He was also recognized by the 14th Dalai Lama. Following many years of study with Buddhist scholars, he began in 1980 to spread the Buddha Dharma, teaching at Karma Kagyu centers throughout the world. Shamar Rinpoche was an accomplished Buddhist master and teacher, respected and cherished the world over.

In 1996, Shamar Rinpoche began organizing Bodhi Path Buddhist Centers, a network of centers covering many continents, in which a non-sectarian approach to meditation is practiced. In addition, over the years, he founded several non-profit organizations worldwide engaged in charitable activities, including projects to provide schooling for children born into poverty, and an organization committed to promoting animal rights.

Shamar Rinpoche encouraged meditation and study among his students, and authored several books for these purposes during his lifetime, including a detailed biographical compilation on the 10th Karmapa, *A Golden Swan in Turbulent Waters* (2012), and a concise meditation guide, *Boundless Awakening: The Heart of Buddhist Meditation* (2013), both published by Bird of Paradise Press. Shamar Rinpoche authored a key text for students, *The Path to Awakening* (Delphinium Books, distributed by Harper Collins, 2014), a presentation of Chekawa Yeshe Dorje's Seven Points of Mind Training, which is both a timely guide to living a fulfilling life as a Buddhist, and a practical manual of meditation techniques. Shamar Rinpoche's instructional book on Mahamudra, *Boundless Wisdom: A Mahāmudrā Practice Manual*, was released in 2018.

About the Contributors

Introduction and glossary by Lama Jampa Thaye

Lama Jampa Thaye is a renowned British scholar and meditation master trained in the Sakya and Kagyu traditions of Buddhism by HH Sakya Trizin, Karma Thinley Rinpoche, and other eminent Tibetan masters. He holds a PhD from the University of Manchester for his work on Tibetan religious history. Lama Jampa Thaye lives in London with his family and maintains an active annual program of teachings for Dechen and other international Buddhist organizations.

Adapted for print by Pamela Gayle White

Pamela Gayle White teaches meditation and Buddhist philosophy in the Americas and Europe, and is one of the Bodhi Path network translator/interpreters. A writer, she has worked closely with many Buddhist masters, notably the 14th Shamarpa, in translating practice texts and commentaries from Tibetan. In addition, Pamela serves as an interfaith hospice chaplain in central Virginia.

Publishing finished
in October 2019 by Pulsio
Publisher Number : 4005
Legal Deposit : October 2019
Printed in Bulgaria